Mountain Home

The Wilderness Poetry of Ancient China

Also by David Hinton

POETRY
Fossil Sky

TRANSLATIONS
The Analects
Chuang Tzu: The Inner Chapters
Mencius
The Mountain Poems of Meng Hao-jan
The Mountain Poems of Hsieh Ling-yün
The Late Poems of Meng Chiao
The Selected Poems of Li Po
The Selected Poems of Po Chü-i
The Selected Poems of T'ao Ch'ien
The Selected Poems of Tu Fu
Tao Te Ching

Mountain Home

The Wilderness Poetry of Ancient China

Selected and Translated by David Hinton

A NEW DIRECTIONS BOOK

Book design by David Bullen Design
Manufactured in the United States of America
New Directions Books are printed on acid-free paper.
First published as a cloth edition by Counterpoint in 2002 and as a New Directions Paperbook (NDP1009) in 2005.
Published simultaneously in Canada by Penguin Books Canada Limited

Library of Congress Cataloging-in-Publication Data

Mountain home : the wilderness poetry of ancient China /
selected and translated by David Hinton.
p. cm.
Originally published: Washington, D.C. : Counterpoint, 2002.
"A new directions book."
Includes bibliographical references and index.
ISBN 0-8112-1624-1 (alk. paper)
1. Chinese poetry—Translations into English. 2. Nature in literature.
I. Title: Wilderness poetry of ancient China. II. Hinton, David, 1954-
PL2658.E3M65 2005
895.1'1008036—dc22   2005000869

New Directions Books are published for James Laughlin
by New Directions Publishing Corporation
80 Eighth Avenue, New York, NY 10011

The translation of this book was supported by grants from the
Charles Engelhard Foundation and the National Endowment for the Arts.

NATIONAL
ENDOWMENT
FOR THE ARTS

Contents

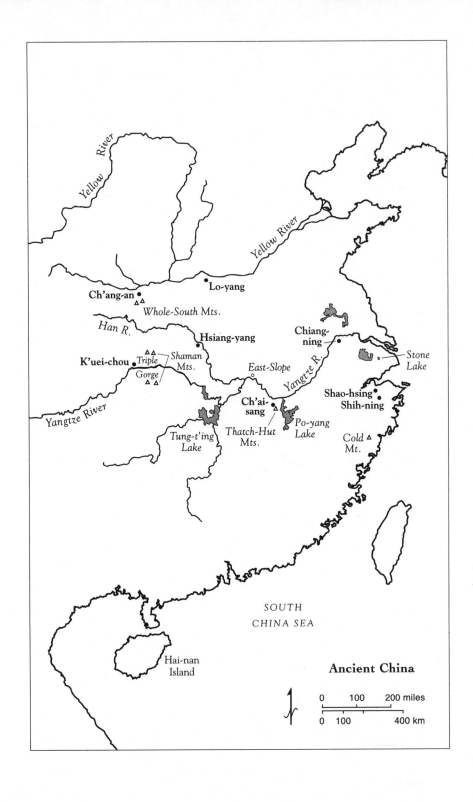

Yellow River

Yellow River

Ch'ang-an •
△ △
Whole-South Mts.

Lo-yang •

Han R.

Hsiang-yang •

Chiang-
ning •

Stone
Lake

K'uei-chou •
△ △
Triple
△ △
Gorge

Shaman
Mts.

East-Slope ◦

Yangtze R.

Shao-hsing •
Shih-ning •

Yangtze River

Ch'ai- •
sang

Po-yang
Lake

Cold △
Mt.

Tung-t'ing
Lake

Thatch-Hut
Mts.

SOUTH
CHINA SEA

Hai-nan
Island

Ancient China

0   100   200 miles

0   100   400 km

Introduction

Originating in the early 5th century C.E. and stretching across two millennia, China's tradition of rivers-and-mountains *(shan-shui)* poetry represents the earliest and most extensive literary engagement with wilderness in human history. Fundamentally different from writing that employs the "natural world" as the stage or materials for human concerns, this poetry articulates a profound and spiritual sense of belonging to a wilderness of truly awesome dimensions. This is not wilderness in the superficial sense of "nature" or "landscape," terms the Western cultural lens has generally applied to this most fundamental aspect of Chinese poetry. "Nature" calls up a false dichotomy between human and nature, and "landscape" suggests a picturesque realm seen from a spectator's distance—but the Chinese wilderness is nothing less than a dynamic cosmology in which humans participate in the most fundamental way.

The poetry of this wilderness cosmology feels utterly contemporary, and in an age of global ecological disruption and mass extinction, this engagement with wilderness makes it more urgently and universally important by the day. But however contemporary this poetry feels, the cosmology that shapes it is not immediately apparent, as this poem by Chia Tao, fairly representative of the rivers-and-mountains tradition, makes clear:

Evening Landscape, Clearing Snow

Walking-stick in hand, I watch snow clear.
Ten thousand clouds and streams banked up,

woodcutters return to their simple homes,
and soon a cold sun sets among risky peaks.

A wildfire burns among ridgeline grasses.
Scraps of mist rise, born of rock and pine.

On the road back to a mountain monastery,
I hear it struck: that bell of evening skies!

The only tangible indication in this poem that suggests the existence of such a cosmology is the monastery. Given the cultural context, it would probably point a Western reader vaguely toward a Ch'an (Zen) Buddhist realm of silence and emptiness. The landscape of the poem does indeed seem infused with that silence and emptiness, a hallmark of Chia Tao's genius, but the poem offers little more than this. That is, of course, as it should be, for the poem naturally operates in the context of its native cosmology and has no reason to explicate its terms. But for us, those terms must be understood before we can begin to read such a poem at depth.

The poem's native cosmology has its source in the originary Taoist masters: Lao Tzu and Chuang Tzu, who lived in the fourth to sixth centuries B.C.E. The central concept in their cosmology is Tao, or Way. *Tao* originally meant "way," as in "pathway" or "roadway," a meaning it has kept. But Lao Tzu and Chuang Tzu redefined it as a spiritual concept by using it to describe the process (hence, a "Way") through which all things arise and pass away. We might approach their Way by speaking of it at its deep ontological level, where the distinction between being *(yu)* and nonbeing *(wu)* arises. Being can be understood in a fairly straightforward way as the empirical universe, the ten thousand living and nonliving things in constant transformation; and nonbeing as the generative void from which this ever-changing realm of being perpetually arises. Within this framework, Way can be understood as a kind of generative ontological process through which all things arise and pass away as nonbeing burgeons forth into the great transformation of being. This is simply an ontological description of natural process, and it is perhaps most immediately manifest in the seasonal cycle: the emptiness of nonbeing in winter, being's burgeoning forth in spring, the fullness of its flourishing in summer, and its dying back into nonbeing in autumn. In their poems, ancient Chinese poets inevitably locate themselves in this cosmology by referring to the seasonal cycle—for as we will see, deep wisdom in ancient China meant dwelling as an organic part of this ontological process.

The mechanism by which being burgeons forth out of nonbeing is *tzu-jan*. The literal meaning of *tzu-jan* is "self-ablaze." From this comes "self-so" or "the of-itself," hence "spontaneous" or "natural." But a more revealing translation of *tzu-jan* might be "occurrence appearing of itself," for it is meant to describe the ten thousand things emerging spontaneously from the generative source, each according to its own nature, independent and self-sufficient, each dying and returning into the process of change, only to reappear in another self-generating form. The poetic significance of this cosmology is especially apparent in the following poem, where the term *tzu-jan* occurs at an archetypal moment in the rivers-and-mountains tradition:

Home Again Among Fields and Gardens

Nothing like all the others, even as a child,
rooted in such love for hills and mountains,

I stumbled into their net of dust, that one
departure a blunder lasting thirteen years.

But a tethered bird longs for its old forest,
and a pond fish its deep waters— so now,

my southern outlands cleared, I nurture
simplicity among these fields and gardens,

home again. I've got nearly two acres here,
and four or five rooms in this thatch hut,

elms and willows shading the eaves in back,
and in front, peach and plum spread wide.

Villages lost across mist-and-haze distances,
kitchen smoke drifting wide-open country,

dogs bark deep among back roads out here,
and roosters crow from mulberry treetops.

No confusion within these gates, no dust,
my empty home harbors idleness to spare.

Back again: after so long caged in that trap,
I've returned to occurrence coming of itself.

This poem was written around 400 C.E. by T'ao Ch'ien, the poet who essentially initiated the Chinese poetic tradition. What makes this poem archetypal is that it tells the story of this "first poet" giving up the empty pursuit of professional ambition and returning home to the more spiritually fulfilling life of a recluse in the mountains. T'ao's return to his farm became a legendary ideal that virtually all later poets and intellectuals revered, and the deeper reason for this is found in the final words of T'ao's poem: "occurrence coming of itself." This term *(tzu-jan)* has traditionally been translated through the lens of Western cultural assumptions as "nature" or "freedom," which reduces this to a kind of sweet pastoral poem, or perhaps a poem of romantic escapism. But this is neither escapism nor sentimental pastoralism: it is a poem about returning to a life in which the perpetual unfolding of Lao Tzu's organic cosmology is the very texture of daily experience.

The vision of *tzu-jan* recognizes earth to be a boundless generative organism, and this vision gives rise to a very different experience of the world. Rather than the metaphysics of time and space, it knows the world as an all-encompassing present, a constant burgeoning forth that includes everything we think of as past and future. It also allows no fundamental distinction between subjective and objective realms, for it includes all that we call mental, all that appears in the mind. And here lies the awesome sense of the sacred in this generative world: for each of the ten thousand things, consciousness among them, seems to be miraculously burgeoning forth from a kind of emptiness at its own heart, and at the same time it is always a burgeoning forth from the very heart of the Cosmos itself.

In fact, the etymology of *yü-chou*, the term that might be translated as "time and space," provides a remarkable view into the cosmology of ancient China. *Yü* (宇) represents *breath spreading free beneath a roof*, from which: *the space beneath eaves*, hence *eaves* or *house*. And by extension it becomes *breath spreading free beneath the canopy of heaven*, from which: *the space beneath the canopy of heaven*, hence *space, space itself as living habitation*. *Chou* (宙) represents *a seed burgeoning forth beneath a roof* (the element beneath the roof being a picture of a seed (由) with a sprout growing out of it), from which: *home*. And by extension it becomes *a seed burgeoning forth, burgeoning steadily forth beneath the canopy of heaven*, from which: *time, time itself as living habitation*. Hence the universe is experienced in its fundamental dimensions as home in the most profound and organic sense.

This cosmology as dwelling-place provided the context for virtually all poetic thinking in ancient China. Indeed, it was central to all Chinese culture, for wilderness has constituted the very terms of self-cultivation throughout the centuries in China. This is most clearly seen in the arts, which were nothing less than spiritual disciplines: calligraphers, poets, and painters aspired to create with the selfless spontaneity of a natural force, and the elements out of which they crafted their artistic visions were primarily aspects of wilderness. It can also be seen, for instance, in the way Chinese intellectuals would sip wine as a way of clarifying awareness of the ten thousand things by dissolving the separation between subject and object, or tea as a way of heightening that awareness, practices that ideally took place outdoors or in an architectural space that was a kind of eye-space, its open walls creating an emptiness that contained the world around it. There is a host of other examples, such as the ideal of living as a recluse among the mountains, or the widespread practice of traveling in areas of particular natural beauty, which generated an extensive travel literature. And as we shall see, meditation was widely practiced as perhaps the most fundamental form of belonging to China's wilderness cosmology.

But the importance of the rivers-and-mountains poetic tradition is not by any means limited to Chinese culture, for it is a poetry suffused in a worldview that is, however foreign, remarkably contemporary and kindred: it is secular, and yet profoundly spiritual; it is thoroughly empirical and basically accords with modern scientific understanding; it is deeply ecological, weaving the human into the "natural world" in the most profound way; and it is radically feminist— a primal cosmology oriented around earth's mysterious generative force and probably deriving in some sense from Paleolithic spiritual practices centered around a Great Mother who continuously gives birth to all things in the unending cycle of life, death, and rebirth.

Within this underlying cosmology, Chia Tao's poem begins to look quite different, and our reading begins to resemble that of its original readers. It is now recognizable as a poem about the experience of attending to the movements of this primal cosmology. The wild mountain realm embodies this cosmology of natural process in its most comprehensive and awesome manifestation. Its basic regions appear almost schematically in countless paintings from the Chinese rivers-and-mountains (also *shan-shui,* but universally translated "landscape") tradition: the pregnant emptiness of nonbeing, in the form of mist and lakes and empty space; the landscape of being as it burgeons forth in a perpetual process of transformation; and then, nestled within this self-generating and harmonious Cosmos, the human. The silence and emptiness that suffuse Chia Tao's landscape are nothing other than nonbeing itself, and the distilled clarity of his images renders the individuating occurrences of *tzu-jan*'s unfolding.

So the poem locates us in the midst of this spiritual ecology of being and nonbeing; then, as mist is born in the third-to-last line (the Chinese believed clouds originated like this in the mountains), the poem moves toward the center of this cosmology, that perpetual moment in which the ten thousand things are generated out of nonbeing. And finally, hearing the sudden call of a bell emerging from the empty silence, ground of both landscape and consciousness, we come to a kind of sudden enlightenment in which we find ourselves there at the very origin of things, in the pregnant emptiness at the heart of this Cosmos.

Invested now with its native cosmology, "Evening Landscape, Clearing Snow" is a very different poem, though the words remain unchanged:

Evening Landscape, Clearing Snow

Walking-stick in hand, I watch snow clear.
Ten thousand clouds and streams banked up,

woodcutters return to their simple homes,
and soon a cold sun sets among risky peaks.

A wildfire burns among ridgeline grasses.
Scraps of mist rise, born of rock and pine.

On the road back to a mountain monastery,
I hear it struck: that bell of evening skies!

*

The wilderness cosmology of ancient China is perhaps most fundamentally alive in the classical Chinese language itself, and its presence there at such deep levels is yet another indication that its origins go back to the earliest cultural levels, levels where Chinese culture and language were just emerging, characters just emerging from hieroglyphs. It is obviously alive in the physicality of the pictographic script, which establishes *tzu-jan*'s ten thousand things as the very medium of consciousness, and so might almost be called the deepest form of Chinese wilderness poetry. And it is no less alive in the verbs, which also manifest the cosmology of *tzu-jan:* rather than embodying a metaphysics of time and space, rather than events in a flow of past, present, and future, the uninflected verbs of classical Chinese simply register action, that steady burgeoning forth of occurrence appearing of itself.

No less remarkable is how the classical Chinese poetic language melds the human into the wilderness cosmology, peopling its grammatical space as sparsely as a grand Sung Dynasty rivers-and-mountains painting. One way this happens is that the language tends to focus on descriptive words, that attention to *tzu-jan,* rather than function words (prepositions and conjunctions) that situate the empirical within human mental constructs. Our function words establish relationships between elements in a poem, but in Chinese those relationships are empty, and must be filled in by the reader. Mostly a list of images, Chia Tao's poem is uncommonly free of these relationships, and this augments the poem's sense of emptiness. But there is one exception that illustrates how these "empty relationships" work: the penultimate line, where in English we cannot avoid subsuming the immediate facts (road, mountains, monastery) to a human mental construction that makes this scene subordinate to the final line. But in Chinese, the elements of the penultimate line's scene are self-apparent:

却	迴	山	寺	路
[contrast]	return	mountain	monastery	road

As even this single line shows, the grammar of this poetic language is minimal in the extreme: meaning determined simply by the order in which words *occur* in an open field. This remarkable openness and ambiguity leaves a great deal unstated: relationships between phrases, ideas, images; temporal location and sequence; very often the subjects and objects of verbal action; and occasionally the verbal action itself. This grammatical openness represents a fundamental shift toward emptiness compared to prose. Hence, the poetic language itself makes poetry a spiritual discipline, and a spiritual discipline shaped by that mysterious generative source at the heart of China's wilderness cosmology. Indeed, the word for poetry (*shih:* 詩) is made up of elements meaning "spoken word" and "temple." The left-hand element meaning "spoken word" portrays sounds coming out of a mouth: 言. And the right-hand element meaning "temple" portrays a hand below (ancient form: 又) that touches seedlings sprouting from the ground (ancient form: 屮): 寺. Hence: "words spoken at the earth altar": 詩. In reading a Chinese poem, you mentally fill in the grammatical emptiness, and yet it always remains emptiness. This means participating in the silence of an empty mind at the boundaries of its true, wordless form, an experience you can know directly in the depths of consciousness through the practice of meditation, the essential activity in the Ch'an monastery that appears at the end of the poem.

In ancient China, meditation was not limited to monks; it was widely practiced by the artist-intellectual class, for it allows us to watch the process of *tzu-jan* in the form of thought burgeoning forth from the emptiness and disappearing back into it. In such meditative practice, we see that we are fundamentally separate from the mental processes we normally identify with, that we are most essentially nothing other than wilderness in the most profound ontological sense. And going deeper into meditative practice, one simply dwells in that undifferentiated emptiness, that generative realm of nonbeing. With this meditative dwelling in the emptiness of nonbeing, we are at the heart of China's wilderness cosmology, inhabiting the primal universe in the most profound way. At this depth, one sees that it is in the ten thousand things that we know ourselves most deeply. As nonbeing, empty mind attends to those ten thousand things with a mirror-like clarity, a spiritual practice that is the very fabric of China's rivers-and-mountains poetry, manifest in its texture of imagistic clarity.

Chia Tao's language, like his mountain landscape, is suffused with the emptiness of nonbeing. But the effect of this is not limited to the absence of verb tenses and function words. In fact, its most dramatic manifestation is the way in which the poet's presence in the poem becomes indistinguishable from that emptiness. Chia Tao's presence is felt at two points in the poem—in the last line, and here in the first:

倚	杖	望	晴	雪
leaning on	walking stick	watch	clearing	snow

As usual in the Chinese poetic language, there is no stated subject in this sentence. Given the introductory clause "Walking-stick in hand," it is clearly the poet who is "watching," although he appears as a kind of emptiness or absence. This sense of selflessness is augmented by the fact that *wang* ("watch") often means "landscape" or "vista" in poems: that which one watches or gazes at. In fact, *wang* appears in the poem's title, and "landscape" is the preferred translation there, though "watch" is also a possibility:

雪	晴	晚	望
snow	clears	evening	landscape ([I] watch)

So the first line might almost be translated as: "Walking-stick in hand :: a landscape of clearing snow."

By the end of the poem, the self has all but vanished:

聞	打	暮	天	鍾
hear	strike	evening	sky	bell

The language in this sentence magically conjures the self as a presence, but it is an utterly empty presence. Here is the Chinese poem as an act of meditative dwelling in the deepest sense. When the bell calls out, we are not only there in the pregnant emptiness at the heart of the Cosmos, we are indistinguishable from it. This dwelling is the Way of ancient China's Taoist and Ch'an sages. In it, self is but a fleeting form taken on by earth's process of change—born out of it, and returned to it in death. Or more precisely, never *out of it:* totally unborn. For those sages, our truest self, being unborn, is all and none of earth's fleeting forms simultaneously. Or more absolutely, it is the emptiness of nonbeing, that source which endures through all change. And ancient China's poets and readers were, in a very real sense, always already masters of this enlightenment, for it is the very structure of their language, their thought, their consciousness. This is utter belonging to a wilderness cosmology as dwelling-place. And as the mountain realm is the most compelling manifestation of this cosmology, it was for them always their mountain home.

Here then is the poem in its final incarnation, beginning to voice all that it can and cannot say in an unenlightened tongue:

Evening Landscape, Clearing Snow

Walking-stick in hand, [I] watch snow clear.
Ten thousand clouds and streams banked up,

woodcutters return to their simple homes,
and soon a cold sun sets among risky peaks.

A wildfire burns among ridgeline grasses.
Scraps of mist rise, born of rock and pine.

[On] the road back to a mountain monastery,
[ ] hear it struck: that bell of evening skies!

Mountain Home

The Wilderness Poetry of Ancient China

Vast and majestic, mountains embrace your shadow;
broad and deep, rivers harbor your voice.

T'AO CH'IEN

Beginnings

(5<small>TH</small> CENTURY C.E.)

T'ao Ch'ien (365–427)

The rise of wilderness poetry in the early 5th century C.E. was part of a profound new engagement with wilderness that arose among Chinese artist-intellectuals for several reasons: the recent loss of northern China to "barbarians," forcing China's artist-intellectuals to emigrate with the government, settling in the southeast where they were enthralled by a new landscape of serenely beautiful mountains; an especially corrupt political culture involving deadly infighting drove many intellectuals to retire into the mountains rather than risk the traditional career of public service; and recent philosophical developments: the revival of Taoist organicist thought, the influx of Buddhist thought from India, and the intermingling of these two traditions, which eventually gave rise to Ch'an (Zen) Buddhism.

Feeling Chinese culture was under siege by the occupying "barbarians," the intellectual class felt a kind of historical imperative to cultivate their tradition and renew it, and most of their epoch-making accomplishments can be seen as part of that new engagement with wilderness. The artistic accomplishments of the age were indeed revolutionary. The origins of Chinese rivers-and-mountains (landscape) painting can be traced to this time, probably beginning as illustrations of rivers-and-mountains poetry. Calligraphy was transformed by the organic spontaneity of Wang Hsi-chih, often called the greatest of Chinese calligraphers, and his no less great son, Wang Hsien-chih. And developments in the field of poetry were perhaps even more dramatic, for the two originary poets of the rivers-and-mountains tradition emerged at this time: T'ao Ch'ien and Hsieh Ling-yün.

Two great anthologies mark the ancient beginnings of the Chinese poetic tradition: the *Shih Ching* (*The Book of Songs*— 10th–6th centuries B.C.E.) and the *Ch'u Tz'u* (*Songs of the South*— 3rd century B.C.E.–2nd century C.E.). But T'ao Ch'ien (T'ao Yüan-ming) was the first writer to make a poetry of his natural voice and immediate experience, thereby creating the personal lyricism that typifies the Chinese tradition. So T'ao Ch'ien effectively stands at the head of the great Chinese poetic tradition like a revered grandfather: profoundly wise, self-possessed, quiet, comforting. And in the quiet resonance of his poetry, a poetry that still speaks today's language, later poets recognized a depth and clarity of wisdom that seemed beyond them.

Born into the educated aristocracy, T'ao was expected to take his proper place in the Confucian order by serving in the government. Accordingly, he took a number of government positions. But he had little patience for the constraints and dangers of official life, and little interest in its superficial rewards, so he finally broke free and returned to the life of a recluse-farmer on the family farm at his ancestral village of Ch'ai-sang (Mulberry-Bramble), just northwest of the famous Thatch-Hut (Lu) Mountain. As mentioned in the general Introduction (p. xv), this was not a romantic return to the bucolic, but to a life in which the spiritual ecology of *tzu-jan* was the very texture of everyday experience. This outline of T'ao Ch'ien's life became a central organizing myth in the Chinese tradition: artist-intellectuals over millennia admired and imitated the way T'ao lived out his life as a recluse, though it meant enduring considerable poverty and hardship (one poem tells of him going into a village to beg for food). And indeed, T'ao's commitment to the recluse life went so deep that he chose "Ch'ien" ("concealed," "hidden," and so: "recluse") as his literary name: Recluse T'ao.

This commitment, so central to the rivers-and-mountains tradition in poetry, was the one honorable alternative to government service for the artist-intellectual class. Already an ancient tradition by T'ao Ch'ien's time, it was a complex political and personal gesture. Politically, it represented a criticism of the government in power: a refusal even to associate with such a government; a model of authenticity and simplicity for those in government whose vanity and greed were so destructive; and, finally, a kind of solidarity with the government's victims among the common people. On the personal level, retirement represented a commitment to a more spiritually fulfilling life in which one inhabits that wilderness cosmology in the most immediate day-to-day way. Such a recluse life did not normally mean living the spartan existence of an ascetic hermit: it was considered the ideal situation for living a broadly civilized life and typically included, along with the wonders of mountain wilderness, a relatively comfortable house, a substantial library, art, wine, family, and friends. And this personal fulfillment had, in turn, clear political dimensions—for the wisdom cultivated in such a recluse life was considered essential to sage governing. Consider this extremely influential passage from the Confucian classic *The Great Learning*:

> In ancient times, wanting to illuminate luminous Integrity in all beneath heaven, they began composing their nation. Wanting to compose their nation, they began putting their families in order. Wanting to put their families in order, they began cultivating themselves. Wanting to cultivate themselves, they began rectifying their minds. Wanting to rectify their minds, they began truing-up their thoughts. Wanting to true-up their thoughts, they began siting their understanding. And to site understanding is to see deep into things themselves.
>
> Once things themselves are seen deeply, understanding is sited.

Once understanding is sited, thought is trued-up. Once thought is trued-up, mind is rectified. Once mind is rectified, self is cultivated. Once self is cultivated, family is in order. Once family is in order, the nation is composed. And once the nation is composed, all beneath heaven is tranquil.

T'ao Ch'ien is traditionally spoken of as founder of the fields-and-gardens tradition, in contrast to Hsieh Ling-yün, founder of the rivers-and-mountains tradition. This is a useful distinction, describing a real difference in emphasis not only in these two originary poets, but throughout the tradition to follow. But there is no fundamental distinction between the two: both embody the cosmology that essentially is the Chinese wilderness, and as rivers-and-mountains is the broader context within which fields-and-gardens operates, it seems more accurate to speak of both modes together as a single rivers-and-mountains tradition.

T'ao Ch'ien's domestic fields-and-gardens feel is more a reflection of his profound contentment than some fundamental difference in his poetic world: unlike Hsieh Ling-yün, whose poems are animated by the need to establish an enlightened relationship with a grand alpine wilderness, T'ao effortlessly lived everyday life on a mountain farm as an utterly sufficient experience of dwelling, his poems initiating that intimate sense of belonging to natural process that shapes the Chinese poetic sensibility. And though this dwelling means confronting death and the existential realities of human experience without delusion, a central preoccupation in T'ao Ch'ien and all Chinese poets, the spiritual ecology of *tzu-jan* provided ample solace. If T'ao's poems seem bland, a quality much admired in them by the Sung Dynasty poets, it's because they are never animated by the struggle for understanding. Instead, they always begin with the deepest wisdom.

After Mulberry-Bramble Liu's Poem

I'd long felt these mountains and lakes
calling, and wouldn't have thought twice,

but my family and friends couldn't bear
talk of living apart. Then one lucky day

a strange feeling came over me and I left,
walking-stick in hand, for my west farm.

No one was going home: on outland roads
farm after farm lay in abandoned ruins,

but our thatch hut's already good as ever,
and our new fields look old and settled.

When valley winds turn bitter and cold
our spring wine eases hunger and work,

and though it isn't strong, just baby-girl
wine, it's better than nothing for worry.

As months and years circle on away here,
the bustling world's ways grown distant,

plowing and weaving provide all we use.
Who needs anything more? Away— away

into this hundred-year life and beyond,
my story and I vanish together like this.

Home Again Among Fields and Gardens

Nothing like all the others, even as a child,
rooted in such love for hills and mountains,

I stumbled into their net of dust, that one
departure a blunder lasting thirteen years.

But a tethered bird longs for its old forest,
and a pond fish its deep waters— so now,

my southern outlands cleared, I nurture
simplicity among these fields and gardens,

home again. I've got nearly two acres here,
and four or five rooms in this thatch hut,

elms and willows shading the eaves in back,
and in front, peach and plum spread wide.

Villages lost across mist-and-haze distances,
kitchen smoke drifting wide-open country,

dogs bark deep among back roads out here,
and roosters crow from mulberry treetops.

No confusion within these gates, no dust,
my empty home harbors idleness to spare.

Back again: after so long caged in that trap,
I've returned to occurrence coming of itself.

After Kuo Chu-pu's Poems

We had warm, wet weather all spring. Now,
white autumn is clear and cold. Dew frozen,

drifting mists gone, bottomless heavens
open over this vast landscape of clarity,

and mountains stretch away, their towering
peaks an unearthly treasure of distance.

These fragrant woodland chrysanthemums
ablaze, green pines lining the clifftops:

isn't this the immaculate heart of beauty,
this frost-deepened austerity? Sipping wine,

I think of recluse masters. A century away,
I nurture your secrets. Your true nature

eludes me here, but taken by quiet, I can
linger this exquisite moon out to the end.

T'ao Ch'ien (365–427)

In Reply to Mulberry-Bramble Liu

In this meager home, guests rare, I often
forget I'm surrounded by turning seasons.

And now falling leaves litter courtyard
emptiness, I grow sadder, realizing it's

autumn already. Fresh sunflower thickets
fill north windows. Sweet grains in south

fields ripen. Though I'm far from happy
today, I know next year may never come.

Get the kids together, I call to my wife,
it's the perfect day for a nice long walk.

Turning Seasons

Turning seasons turning wildly
away, morning's majestic calm

unfolds. Out in spring clothes,
I roam eastern fields. Lingering

clouds sweep mountains clean.
Gossamer mist blurs open skies.

And soon, feeling south winds,
young grain ripples like wings.

T'ao Ch'ien (365–427)

Drinking Wine

5

I live here in a village house without
all that racket horses and carts stir up,

and you wonder how that could ever be.
Wherever the mind dwells apart is itself

a distant place. Picking chrysanthemums
at my east fence, I see South Mountain

far off: air lovely at dusk, birds in flight
returning home. All this means something,

something absolute: whenever I start
to explain it, I forget words altogether.

7

Color infusing autumn chrysanthemums
exquisite, I pick dew-bathed petals,

float them on that forget-your-cares
stuff. Even my passion for living apart

grows distant. I'm alone here, and still
the winejar soon fills cups without me.

Everything at rest, dusk: a bird calls,
returning to its forest home. Chanting,

I settle into my breath. Somehow, on this
east veranda, I've found my life again.

T'ao Ch'ien (365–427)

Wandering at Oblique Creek

This new year makes it fifty suddenly
gone. Thinking of life's steady return

to rest cuts deep, driving me to spend
all morning wandering. Skies clear,

air's breath fresh, I sit with friends
beside this stream flowing far away.

Striped bream weave gentle currents;
calling gulls drift above idle valleys.

Eyes roaming distant waters, I find
ridge above ridge: it's nothing like

majestic nine-fold immortality peaks,
but to reverent eyes it's incomparable.

Taking the winejar, I pour a round,
and we start offering brimful toasts:

who knows where today might lead
or if all this will ever come true again.

After a few cups, my heart's far away,
and I forget thousand-year sorrows:

ranging to the limit of this morning's
joy, it isn't tomorrow I'm looking for.

An Idle 9/9 at Home

9th day 9th Month
Ever & Ever

Life too short for so many lasting desires,
people adore immortality. When the months

return to this day of promise, everyone
fondly hears *ever and ever* in its name.

Warm winds have ended. Dew ice-cold,
stars blaze in crystalline skies. And now

swallows have taken their shadows south,
arriving geese keep calling and calling.

Wine eases worry, and chrysanthemums
keep us from the ruins of age, but if you

live in a bramble hut, helplessly watching
these turning seasons crumble— what then?

My empty winejar shamed by a dusty cup,
this cold splendor of blossoms opens for itself

alone. I tighten my robe and sing to myself,
idle, overwhelmed by each memory. So many

joys to fill a short stay. I'll take my time
here. It is whole. How could it be any less?

Cha *Festival Day*

Seeing off the year's final day, windblown
snow can't slow this warm weather. Already,

at our gate planted with plum and willow,
there's a branch flaunting lovely blossoms.

When I chant, words come clear. And in wine
I touch countless distances. So much still

eludes me here— who knows how much when
there's such unearthly Manifest Mountain song?

Written One Morning in the 5th Moon, After Tai Chu-pu's Poem

It's all an empty boat, oars dangling free,
but return goes on without end. The year

begins, and suddenly, in a moment's glance,
midyear stars come back around, bright

sun and moon bringing all things to such
abundance. North woods lush, blossoming,

rain falls in season from hallowed depths.
Dawn opens. Summer breezes rise. No one

comes into this world without leaving soon.
It's our inner pattern, which never falters.

At home here in what lasts, I wait out life.
A bent arm my pillow, I keep empty whole.

Follow change through rough and smooth,
and life's never up or down. If you can see

how much height fills whatever you do, why
climb Hua or Sung, peaks of immortality?

T'ao Ch'ien (365–427)

Untitled

Days and months never take their time.
The four seasons keep bustling each other

away. Cold winds churn lifeless branches.
Fallen leaves cover long paths. We're frail,

crumbling more with each turning year.
Our temples turn white early, and once

your hair flaunts that bleached streamer,
the road ahead starts closing steadily in.

This house is an inn awaiting travelers,
and I yet another guest leaving. All this

leaving and leaving— where will I ever
end up? My old home's on South Mountain.

Hsieh Ling-yün (385–433)

As a patriarch of perhaps the wealthiest and most powerful family in China, Hsieh Ling-yün was deeply involved in the turbulent political world for decades, but he was a mountain recluse at heart. When he was eventually exiled, finding himself in a period of quiet reflection at a beautiful site on a mountainous seacoast in southeast China, he underwent a kind of Buddhist awakening to wilderness. As a result, he abandoned politics and retired to his family home high in the mountains at Shih-ning—a move that he speaks of, like T'ao Ch'ien, as a return to "the sacred beauty of *tzu-jan*" (p. 25). And though he is traditionally considered the great originator of the wild rivers-and-mountains mode, many of his finest poems are oriented around the fields-and-gardens landscape of his family estate.

At the time of his awakening, Hsieh wrote an essay that is considered the earliest surviving Ch'an text in China, and its ideas provide a framework for his poetry, and for much of the rivers-and-mountains poetry to follow. It describes enlightenment as becoming the emptiness of nonbeing, and as such, mirroring being as it unfolds according to the *inner pattern* (see Key Terms: *li*), a key concept that recurs often in Hsieh's poetry and throughout the wilderness tradition. The philosophical meaning of *li*, which originally referred to the veins and markings in a precious piece of jade, is something akin to what we call natural law. It is the system of principles according to which the ten thousand things burgeon forth spontaneously from the generative void. For Hsieh, one comes to a deep understanding of *li* through *adoration (shang)*, another recurring concept in the poems (pp. 24, 36). *Adoration* denotes an aesthetic experience of the wild mountain realm as a single overwhelming whole. It is this aesthetic experience that Hsieh's poems try to evoke in the reader, this sense of inhabiting that wilderness cosmology in the most profound way.

As with China's great rivers-and-mountains paintings, Hsieh's mountain landscapes enact "nonbeing mirroring the whole" (empty mind mirroring the whole), rendering a world that is deeply spiritual and, at the same time, resolutely realistic. Here lies the difficulty Hsieh's work presents to a reader. It is an austere poetry, nearly devoid of the human stories and poetic strategies that normally make poems engaging. Hsieh's central personal "story" is the identification of enlightenment with wilderness, and this is precisely why Hsieh has been so admired in China. Rendering the day-to-day adventure of a person inhabiting the universe at great depth, Hsieh's poems tend more to the descriptive and philosophical, locating human consciousness in its primal relation to the Cosmos. In so doing, they replace narrow human concerns with a mirror-still mind that sees its truest self in the vast and complex dimensions of mountain wilderness. But as there was no fundamental distinction between mind and heart in ancient China (see Key Terms: *hsin*), this was a profound emotional experience as well, and it remains so for us today. With their grandiose language, headlong movement, and shifting perspective, Hsieh's poems were especially celebrated for possessing an elemental power which captures the dynamic spirit and inner rhythms that infuse the numinous realm of rivers and mountains; and reading them requires that you participate in his mirror-still dwelling. Hsieh's great poems may seem flat at first, and very much alike—but in that dwelling, each day is another form of enlightenment, and each walk another walk at the very heart of the Cosmos itself.

On a Tower Beside the Lake

Quiet mystery of lone dragons alluring,
calls of migrant geese echoing distances,

I meet sky, unable to soar among clouds,
face a river, all those depths beyond me.

Too simple-minded to perfect Integrity
and too feeble to plow fields in seclusion,

I followed a salary here to the sea's edge
and lay watching forests bare and empty.

That sickbed kept me blind to the seasons,
but opening the house up, I'm suddenly

looking out, listening to surf on a beach
and gazing up into high mountain peaks.

A warm sun is unraveling winter winds,
new *yang* swelling, transforming old *yin*.

Lakeshores newborn into spring grasses
and garden willows become caroling birds:

in them the ancient songs haunt me with
flocks and flocks and *full lush and green.*

Isolate dwelling so easily becomes forever.
It's hard settling the mind this far apart,

but not something ancients alone master:
that serenity is everywhere apparent here.

Hsieh Ling-yün (385–433)

Climbing Green-Cliff Mountain in Yung-chia

Taking a little food, a light walking-stick,
I wander up to my home in quiet mystery,

the path along streams winding far away
onto ridgetops, no end to this wonder at

slow waters silent in their frozen beauty
and bamboo glistening at heart with frost,

cascades scattering a confusion of spray
and broad forests crowding distant cliffs.

Thinking it's moonrise I see in the west
and sunset I'm watching blaze in the east,

I hike on until dark, then linger out night
sheltered away in deep expanses of shadow.

Immune to high importance: that's renown.
Walk humbly and it's all promise in beauty,

for in quiet mystery the way runs smooth,
ascending remote heights beyond compare.

Utter tranquillity, the distinction between
yes this and *no that* lost, I embrace primal

unity, thought and silence woven together,
that deep healing where we venture forth.

I've Put in Gardens South of the Fields, Opened Up a Stream and Planted Trees

Woodcutter and recluse— they inhabit
these mountains for different reasons,

and there are other forms of difference.
You can heal here among these gardens,

sheltered from rank vapors of turmoil,
wilderness clarity calling distant winds.

I *ch'i*-sited my house on a northern hill,
doors opening out onto a southern river,

ended trips to the well with a new stream
and planted hibiscus in terraced banks.

Now there are flocks of trees at my door
and crowds of mountains at my window,

and I wander thin trails down to fields
or gaze into a distance of towering peaks,

wanting little, never wearing myself out.
It's rare luck to make yourself such a life,

though like ancient recluse paths, mine
bring longing for the footsteps of friends:

how could I forget them in this exquisite
adoration kindred spirits alone can share?

Hsieh Ling-yün (385–433)

Dwelling in the Mountains

4

Embracing the seasons of heaven through bright insight,
the impulse turning them, and the inner pattern's solitude,

my grandfather came to this retreat in the dusk of old age,
leaving behind his renown engraved in memorial hymns.

He thought Ch'ü Yüan a fool for drowning himself in exile,
admired Yüeh Yi for leaving his country. And he himself—

choosing the sacred beauty of occurrence coming of itself,
he made the composure of these mountain peaks his own.

5

Looking up to the example that old sage handed down,
and considering what comes easily to my own nature,

I offered myself to this tranquil repose of dwelling,
and now nurture my lifework in the drift of idleness.

Master Pan's early awakening always humbled me,
and I was shamed by Master Shang's old-age insight,

so with years and sickness both closing in upon me
I devoted myself to simplicity and returned to it all,

left that workaday life for this wisdom of wandering,
for this wilderness of rivers-and-mountains clarity.

Hsieh Ling-yün (385–433)

6

Here where I live,
lakes on the left, rivers on the right,
you leave islands, follow shores back

to mountains out front, ridges behind.
Looming east and toppling aside west,

they harbor ebb and flow of breath,
arch across and snake beyond, devious

churning and roiling into distances,
clifftop ridgelines hewn flat and true.

7

Nearby in the east are
Risen-Fieldland and Downcast-Lake,
Western-Gorge and Southern-Valley,

Stone-Plowshares and Stone-Rapids,
Forlorn-Millstone and Yellow-Bamboo.

There are waters tumbling a thousand feet in flight
and forests curtained high over countless canyons,

endless streams flowing far away into distant rivers
and cascades branching deeper into nearby creeks.

Hsieh Ling-yün (385—433)

12

Far off to the south are
peaks like Pine-Needle and Nest-Hen,
Halcyon-Knoll and Brimmed-Stone,

Harrow and Spire Ridges faced together,
Elder and Eye-Loft cleaving summits.

When you go deep, following a winding river to its source,
you're soon bewildered, wandering a place beyond knowing:

cragged peaks towering above stay lost in confusions of mist,
and depths sunken away far below surge and swell in a blur.

24

There are fish like
snake-fish and trout, perch and tench,
red-eye and yellow-gill, dace and carp,

bream, sturgeon, skate, mandarin-fish,
flying-fish, bass, mullet and wax-fish:

a rainbow confusion of colors blurred,
glistening brocade, cloud-fresh schools

nibbling duckweed, frolicking in waves,
drifting among ghost-eye, flowing deep.

Some drumming their gills and leaping through whitewater,
others beating their tails and struggling back beneath swells,

shad and salmon, each in their season, stream up into creeks and shallows,
sunfish and knife-fish follow rapids further, emerge in mountain springs.

Hsieh Ling-yün (385–433)

26

On mountaintops live
gibbon, jackal, wildcat and badger,
fox and wolf, cougar and bobcat,

and in mountain valleys
black and brown bear, coyote, tiger,
bighorn and deer, antelope and elk.

Things gambol among branches soaring out over cliffs
and leap across rifts of empty sky within deep gorges,

lurk down through valleys, howls and roars perpetual,
while others climb, calling and wailing among treetops.

33

As for my
homes perched north and south,
inaccessible except across water:

gaze deep into wind and cloud
and you know this realm utterly.

Hsieh Ling-yün (385–433)

36

Tracing the way back home here,
I might round North Mountain

on roads hung along cliffwalls,
timbers rising in switchbacks,

or I could take the watercourse
way winding and circling back,

level lakes broad and brimming,
crystalline depths clear and deep

beyond shorelines all lone grace
and long islands of lush brocade.

Gazing on and on in reverence
across realms so boundless away,

I come to the twin rivers that flow through together.
Two springs sharing one source,

they follow gorges and canyons
to merge at mountain headlands

and cascade on, scouring sand out and mounding dunes
below peaks that loom over islands swelling into hills,

whitewater carrying cliffs away in a tumble of rocks,
a marshy tangle of fallen trees glistening in the waves.

Following along the south bank that crosses out front,
the snaking north cliff that looms behind, I'm soon

lost in thick forests, the nature of dusk and dawn in full view,
and for bearings, I trust myself to the star-filled night skies.

On Stone-Gate Mountain's Highest Peak

I started thinking of impossible cliffs at dawn
and by evening was settled on a mountaintop,

scarcely a peak high enough to face this hut
looking out on mountains veined with streams,

forests stretching away beyond its open gate,
a tumble of talus boulders ending at the stairs.

Mountains crowd around, blocking out roads,
and trails wander bamboo confusions, leaving

guests to stray on clever new paths coming up
or doubt old ways leading people back home.

Hissing cascades murmuring through dusk,
the wail of gibbons howling away the night,

I keep to the inner pattern, deep in meditation,
and nurturing this Way, never wander amiss.

Mind now a twin to stark late autumn trees
while eyes delight in the flowering of spring,

I inhabit the constant and wait out the end,
content to dwell at ease in all change and loss,

in this regret there's no kindred spirit here
to climb this ladder of azure clouds with me.

Overnight at Stone-Gate Cliffs

I spent the morning digging out orchids,
afraid frost would soon leave them dead,

passed the night among fringes of cloud,
savoring a moon up beyond all this rock,

chortles telling me birds have settled in,
falling leaves giving away fresh winds.

Sounds weave together in the ear, strange
unearthly echoes all crystalline distance,

though there's no one to share wonders
or the joys in wine's fragrant clarities.

We'll never meet again now. I sit beside
a stream, sun drying my hair for nothing.

Following Axe-Bamboo Stream, I Cross
Over a Ridge and Hike on Along the River

Though the cry of gibbons means sunrise,
its radiance hasn't touched this valley all

quiet mystery. Clouds gather below cliffs,
and there's still dew glistening on blossoms

when I set out along a wandering stream,
climbing into narrow canyons far and high.

Ignoring my robe to wade through creeks,
I scale cliff-ladders and cross distant ridges

to the river beyond. It snakes and twists,
but I follow it, happy just meandering along

past pepperwort and duckweed drifting deep,
rushes and wild rice in crystalline shallows.

Reaching tiptoe to ladle sips from waterfalls
and picking still unfurled leaves in forests,

I can almost see that lovely mountain spirit
in a robe of fig leaves and sash of wisteria.

Gathering orchids brings no dear friends
and picking hemp-flower no open warmth,

but the heart finds its beauty in adoration,
and you can't talk out such shadowy things:

in the eye's depths you're past worry here,
awakened into things all wandering away.

Hsieh Ling-yün (385–433)

On Thatch-Hut Mountain

. . .

Above jumbled canyons opening suddenly
out and away, level roads all breaking off,

these thronging peaks nestle up together.
People come and go without a trace here,

sun and moon hidden all day and night,
frost and snow falling summer and winter.

. . .

scale cliffwalls to gaze into dragon pools
and climb trees to peer into nursery dens.

. . .

no imagining mountain visits. And now
I can't get enough, just walk on and on,

and even a single dusk and dawn up here
shows you the way through empty and full.

. . .

Hsieh Ling-yün (385–433)   *37*

In Hsin-an, Setting Out from the River's Mouth at T'ung-lu

Cold cutting through thin openwork robes
and not yet time for gifts of winter clothes:

this season always pitches me into depths
all grief-clotted thoughts of ancient times.

I'll never sail on thousand-mile oars again
or think through the hundred generations,

but Master Shang's distant mind my own
now, and old Master Hsü's recluse ways,

I wander these winds boundless and clear,
and the headlong rush of autumn streams.

Rivers and mountains open away through
that alluring luster cloud and sun share,

and when twilight's clarity infuses it all,
I savor a joy things themselves know here.

T'ang Dynasty

(618–907)

Meng Hao-jan (689–740)

Unlike T'ao Ch'ien and Hsieh Ling-yün, who settled into their recluse ways later in life, Meng Hao-jan never left his home mountains to follow a government career. Meng traveled extensively, making all China his neighborhood landscape, but his home remained always in Hsiang-yang, a region known for its lovely mountains towering above the Han River. In ancient China, a person's home landscape was generally thought to have a profound influence on their character, and Meng was so closely associated with Hsiang-yang that it became his posthumous name: Meng Hsiang-yang. Meng lived at a number of secluded mountain locations in Hsiang-yang (most famously, Deer-Gate Mountain). Meng also explored the area extensively, often hiking its mountains and valleys, paddling its rivers and lakes. And indeed, his character seems to have been shaped by this intimacy: he became legendary for possessing the protean freedom of Hsiang-yang's rivers and mountains. In this he resembles Hsieh Ling-yün, a resemblance reflected in his poetry as well. But although it shares Hsieh's rambling exuberance, Meng's poetry enriched it with a new subjective dimension.

After T'ao Ch'ien and Hsieh Ling-yün, Chinese poetry was generally mired in lifeless convention until the T'ang Dynasty three centuries later, when poetry blossomed into its first full splendor. And a major catalyst in the T'ang renaissance was admiration for T'ao and Hsieh, who had been neglected since their deaths. During this hiatus, Ch'an Buddhism came to maturity and became widely practiced among the intelligentsia of China. Ch'an not only clarified anew the spiritual ecology of early Taoist thought, it also emphasized the old Taoist idea that deep understanding lies beyond words. In poetry, this gave rise to a much more distilled language, especially in its concise imagism (empty mind mirroring *tzu-jan*), which opened new inner depths, nonverbal insights, and even outright enigma. This enigma and imagistic concision opens the poem to silence; and as with meditation, this silence is itself wilderness, the non-verbal and non-human. So this new poetics weaves consciousness into wilderness, making this weave the very texture of poetic experience. It was in the work of Meng Hao-jan, the first great T'ang Dynasty poet, that this poetic revolution began. And although later poets developed this new aesthetic further, there is a sense in which Meng remained its most radical exemplar: it is said that he destroyed most poems after writing them because he didn't feel words could capture his intent. Those poems survive as silence, that most perfect literary embodiment of wilderness.

Gathering Firewood

Gathering firewood I enter mountain depths,
mountain depths rising creek beyond creek

choked with the timbers of bridges in ruins.
Vines tumble low, tangled over cragged paths,

and at dusk, scarce people grow scarcer still.
Mountain wind sweeping through simple robes,

my chant steady, I shoulder a light bundle,
watch smoke drift across open country home.

Sent to Ch'ao, the Palace Reviser

You polish words in rue-scented libraries,
and I live in bamboo-leaf gardens, a recluse

wandering every day the same winding path
home to rest in the quiet, no noise anywhere.

A bird soaring the heights can choose a tree,
but the hedge soon tangles impetuous goats.

Today, things seen becoming thoughts felt:
this is where you start forgetting the words.

Autumn Begins

Autumn begins unnoticed. Nights slowly lengthen,
and little by little, clear winds turn colder and colder,

summer's blaze giving way. My thatch hut grows still.
At the bottom stair, in bunchgrass, lit dew shimmers.

Traveling to Yüeh, I Linger Out Farewell with Chang and Shen of Ch'iao District

This morning I set off down the Pien Canal
and tonight stop over on the border of Ch'iao,

full of joy because this west wind has blown
us together here, old friends meeting again.

You'll stay, perfecting Mei Fu's recluse way,
and I'll set out following the hermit Po Lüan.

After this farewell, we'll think of each other
anytime: clouds drift twin lands Wu and Kuei.

Overnight at Cypress-Peak Monastery on Heaven-Terrace Mountain

Trusting wind-filled sails to travel the seas,
I lingered out nights along islands of cloud,

roamed isle-of-immortality joys far and wide,
and came to the splendor of red-wall cliffs.

Clutching vines and stepping out onto moss
there, I left my oars and set out to explore,

then settled among shadows at Cypress-Peak,
blossoms and mushroom cures everywhere,

cranes calling out through dew-fall clarity,
roosters crying across an aimless early tide.

No interest in the fetters of responsibility,
I leave all worry and trouble behind here,

wander the heights onto Radiant-Four Ridge,
follow dark-enigma to Primal-Three Canyon,

and soon, lost deep in thoughts all distant
wandering, perfecting that deathless Way,

I'm looking across three twilight mountains,
clouds billowing empty and boundless away.

Anchored Off Hsün-yang in Evening Light, I Gaze at Thatch-Hut Mountain's Incense-Burner Peak

Our sail up full, thousands of miles pass
without meeting mountains of renown,

then anchored here outside Hsün-yang,
I'm suddenly gazing at Incense-Burner.

I've always read Hui Yüan's teachings,
traced his pure path beyond the dust,

and now his East-Forest home is so near.
It is dusk. A bell sounds, and it's empty.

Anchored Overnight on Thatch-Hut River and Hearing Old Friends Are Staying at East-Forest Monastery, I Send This Poem

On this river skirting Thatch-Hut Mountain,
where Pine-Gate Stream enters Tiger Creek,

I hear you're passing the clear night there
at East-Forest, exploring the joys of stillness.

Here, fearful doves roosting in *ch'an* forests,
mountain purity uneasy in Stone-Mirror rock,

this lone lamp is itself that awakened Way:
it lights a traveler's mind past all confusion.

On a Journey to Thought-Essence Monastery, Inscribed on the Wall of the Abbot's Mountain Hut

Happening into realms peach-blossom pure,
I begin to feel the depths of a bamboo path,

and soon come to know a master's timeless
dwelling. It's far beyond things people seek.

Cranes dancing over steps all stone idleness,
gibbons in flight howling amid thick forests,

I slowly fathom dark-enigma's inner pattern,
and sitting at such depths, forget mind itself.

Climbing Deer-Gate Mountain,
Thoughts of Ancient Times

Driven by dawn's bright clarity, I set out
riding currents past riverside mountains,

shorebirds coming into view, close, clear,
and shoreline trees blurring away behind.

Then slower as I reach Deer-Gate Mountain,
mountain a bright haze of kingfisher-green,

I paddle twisted pools meandering cliff-walls,
my wandering boat snaking in and around.

Legend speaks of Master P'ang, that recluse
who came for herbs and stayed on, tending

mushroom and thistle along golden streams,
sleeping on a stone bed of lichen and moss.

And lost in thoughts of that long-ago sage,
I put my boat ashore and hike up to where

traces of his recluse home still stand today.
In this wind at the far end of distance now,

his timeless cinnamons regal and empty,
he's white cloud that one day drifted away.

And soon, thoughts searching on and on,
my boat's floating home through dusk light.

Returning Home to Deer-Gate Mountain at Night

As day fades into dusk, the bell at a mountain temple sounds.
Fish-Bridge Island is loud with people clamoring at the ferry,

and others follow sandy shores toward their river village.
But returning home to Deer-Gate, I paddle my own little boat,

Deer-Gate's incandescent moonlight opening misty forests,
until suddenly I've entered old Master P'ang's isolate realm.

Cliffs the gate, pines the path— it's forever still and silent,
just this one recluse, this mystery coming and going of itself.

Looking for the Recluse Chang Tzu-jung on White-Crane Cliff

On a trail atop White-Crane's blue cliffs,
my recluse friend's at home in solitude,

step and courtyard empty water and rock.
Forest and creek free of axe and fish trap,

months and years turn young pines old,
wind and frost keep bitter bamboo sparse.

Gazing deep, I embrace ancestral ways,
set out wandering toward my simple hut.

Visiting the Hermitage of Ch'an Monk Jung

In the mountaintop meditation room, just a monk's robes.
And outside windows, no one. Birds at the stream take flight.

Yellow dusk stretching half-way down the mountain road,
I hear cascades in love with kingfisher-greens gone dark.

Looking for Mei, Master of Way

The willows of a master shading this lake,
and his geese afloat in mountain shadows:

come following all I adore up to countless
summer clouds, I leave my walking-stick,

and echoing the joy seen in drifting fish,
set out on the song of a drumming paddle.

The regal path of high peaks never falters:
a thousand years bowing into clear waters.

At Lumen-Empty Monastery, Visiting the Hermitage of Master Jung, My Departed Friend

The blue-lotus roof standing beside a pond,
White-Horse Creek tumbling through forests,

and my old friend some strange thing now.
A lingering visitor, alone and grief-stricken

after graveside rites among pines, I return,
looking for your sitting-mat spread on rock.

Bamboo that seems always my own thoughts:
it keeps fluttering here at your thatch hut.

Climbing South-View Mountain's Highest Peak

Rivers and mountains beyond the form seen:
Hsiang-yang's beauty brings them in reach,

and South-View has the highest peak around.
Somehow I never climbed its cragged heights,

its rocky cliffs like walls hacked and scraped
and towering over mountains crowded near,

but today, skies so bright and clear, I set out.
Soon the far end of sight's all boundless away,

Cloud-Dream southlands a trifle in the palm,
Savage-Knoll lost in that realm of blossoms.

And back on my horse, riding home at dusk,
a vine-sifted moon keeps the stream lit deep.

Meng Hao-jan (689–740)

Wang Wei (701–761)

Wang Wei may be China's most immediately appealing poet, and historically he was no less revered as a painter. Rather than rendering a realistic image of a landscape, Wang is traditionally spoken of as the first to paint the inner spirit of landscape; and since this became the essence of Chinese rivers-and-mountains painting as it blossomed in the following centuries, he must be counted as one of the great originators in the rivers-and-mountains tradition. This ability to capture a kind of inexpressible inner spirit is also the essence of Wang's poetry. He developed a tranquil rivers-and-mountains poem that dramatically extends Meng Hao-jan's poetics of enigma, wherein the poem goes far beyond the words on the page, and deepens Meng's opening into silence that weaves consciousness into wilderness. As with Meng Hao-jan, this poetics can be traced to Wang Wei's assiduous practice of Ch'an Buddhism. The sense that deep understanding is enigmatic and beyond words is central to Ch'an; and it is the silent emptiness of meditation, Ch'an's way of fathoming that wordless enigma, that gives Wang's poems their resounding tranquillity.

Wang Wei's poetry is especially celebrated for the way he could make himself disappear into a landscape, and so dwell as belonging utterly to China's wilderness cosmology. In Ch'an practice, the self and its constructions of the world dissolve away until nothing remains but empty mind or "no-mind." Beginning with Hsieh Ling-yün, the Ch'an tradition spoke of this empty mind as mirroring the world, leaving its ten thousand things utterly simple, utterly themselves, and utterly sufficient. Wang Wei's brief poems resound with the selfless clarity of no-mind, and in them the simplest image resonates with the whole cosmology of *tzu-jan*. It is an egoless poetry, one that renders the ten thousand things in such a way that they empty the self as they shimmer with the clarity of their own self-sufficient identity.

Mourning Meng Hao-jan

My dear friend nowhere in sight,
this Han River keeps flowing east.

Now, if I look for old masters here,
I find empty rivers and mountains.

In Reply to P'ei Ti

The cold river spreads boundless away.
Autumn rains darken azure-deep skies.

You ask about Whole-South Mountain:
the mind knows beyond white clouds.

Wheel-Rim River Sequence

1 Elder-Cliff Cove

At the mouth of Elder-Cliff, a rebuilt house
among old trees, broken remnants of willow.

Those to come: who will they be, their grief
over someone's long-ago life here empty.

2 Master-Flourish Ridge

Birds in flight go on leaving and leaving.
And autumn colors mountain distances again:

crossing Master-Flourish Ridge and beyond,
is there no limit to all this grief and sorrow?

3 *Apricot-Grain Cottage*

Roofbeams cut from deep-grained apricot,
fragrant reeds braided into thatched eaves:

no one knows clouds beneath these rafters
drifting off to bring that human realm rain.

4 *Bamboo-Clarity Mountains*

Tall bamboo blaze in meandering emptiness:
kingfisher-green rippling streamwater blue.

On Autumn-Pitch Mountain roads, they flaunt
such darkness, woodcutters too beyond knowing.

5 *Deer Park*

No one seen. In empty mountains,
hints of drifting voice, no more.

Entering these deep woods, late sunlight ablaze on green moss, rising.

6 *Magnolia Park*

Autumn mountains gathering last light,
one bird follows another in flight away.

Shifting kingfisher-greens flash radiant
scatters. Evening mists: nowhere they are.

8 *Scholartree Path*

On the side path shaded by scholartrees,
green moss fills recluse shadow. We still

keep it swept, our welcome at the gate,
knowing a mountain monk may stop by.

10 *South Lodge*

I leave South Lodge, boat light, water
so vast you never reach North Lodge.

Far shores: I see villagers there beyond
knowing in all this distance, distance.

11 *Vagary Lake*

Flute-song carries beyond furthest shores.
In dusk light, I bid you a sage's farewell.

Across this lake, in the turn of a head,
mountain greens furl into white clouds.

13 *Golden-Rain Rapids*

Wind buffets and blows autumn rain.
Water cascading thin across rocks,

waves lash at each other. An egret
startles up, white, then settles back.

15 *White-Rock Shallows*

White-Rock Shallows open and clear,
green reeds past prime for harvest:

families come down east and west,
rinse thin silk radiant in moonlight.

16 *North Lodge*

At North Lodge north of these lakewaters,
railings flash red through tangled trees.

Here, meandering forest-stained horizons,
South River shimmers in and out of view.

17 *Bamboo-Midst Cottage*

Sitting alone in recluse bamboo dark
I play a *ch'in,* settle into breath chants.

In these forest depths, no one knows
this moon come bathing me in light.

18 *Magnolia Slope*

Waterlily blossoms out on tree branches
flaunt crimson calyces among mountains.

At home beside this stream, quiet, no one
here. Scattered. Scattered open and falling.

In the Mountains, Sent to Ch'an Brothers and Sisters

Dharma companions filling mountains,
a sangha forms of itself: chanting, sitting

ch'an stillness. Looking out from distant
city walls, people see only white clouds.

In Reply to Su, Who Visited My Wheel-Rim River Hermitage When I Wasn't There to Welcome Him

I live humbly near the canyon's mouth
where stately trees ring village ruins.

When you came on twisted rocky paths,
who welcomed you at my mountain gate?

Fishing boats frozen into icy shallows,
hunting fires out across cold headlands,

and in all this quiet beyond white clouds,
wild gibbons heard among distant bells.

Mourning Yin Yao

Returning you to Stone-Tower Mountain, we bid farewell
among ash-green pine and cypress, then return home.

Of your bones now buried white cloud, this much remains
forever: streams cascading empty toward human realms.

Bird-Cry Creek

In our idleness, cinnamon blossoms fall.
In night quiet, spring mountains stand

empty. Moonrise startles mountain birds:
here and there, cries in a spring gorge.

Adrift on the Lake

Autumn sky illuminates itself all empty
distances away toward far human realms,

cranes off horizons of sand tracing its
clarity into mountains beyond clouds.

Crystalline waters quiet settling night.
Moonlight leaving idleness everywhere

ablaze, I trust myself to this lone paddle,
this calm on and on, no return in sight.

On Returning to Wheel-Rim River

At the canyon's mouth, a far-off bell stirs.
Woodcutters and fishermen scarcer still,

sunset distant in these distant mountains,
I verge on white clouds, returning alone.

Frail water-chestnut vines never settle,
and light cottonwood blossoms fly easily.

Spring grass coloring the east ridge, all
ravaged promise, I close my bramble gate.

In Reply to Vice-Magistrate Chang

In these twilight years, I love tranquillity
alone. Mind free of our ten thousand affairs,

self-regard free of all those grand schemes,
I return to my old forest, knowing empty.

Soon mountain moonlight plays my *ch'in*.
Pine winds loosen my robes. Explain this

inner pattern behind failure and success?
Fishing song carries into shoreline depths.

Li Po (701–762)

There is a set-phrase in Chinese referring to the phenomenon of Li Po: "Winds of the immortals, bones of the Way." He is called the "Banished Immortal," an exiled spirit moving through this world with an unearthly ease and freedom from attachment. But at the same time, he belongs to earth in the most profound way, for he is also free of attachments to self, and that allows him to blend easily into a weave of identification with *tzu-jan*'s process of change: that spontaneous burgeoning forth of the ten thousand things.

Li Po's work is suffused with the wonder of being part of this process, but at the same time he enacts it, makes it visible in the self-dramatized spontaneity of his life and work. Li's life was characterized by whimsical travel, wild drinking, and a gleeful disdain for decorum and authority. This spontaneity is also central to Li Po's experience of the natural world. He is primarily engaged by the natural world in its wild, rather than domestic, forms. Not only does the wild evoke wonder, it is also where the spontaneous energy of *tzu-jan*, energy with which Li Po identified, is clearly visible. And the headlong movement of a Li Po poem literally enacts this identification, this belonging to earth in the fundamental sense of belonging to its processes.

Li Po's spontaneous energy is finally nothing other than the unfolding of being, which is rooted in the profound stillness of nonbeing, a stillness often found in his more meditative poems. And according to legend, when the phenomenon of Li Po returned in the end to that stillness of nonbeing, it too was an event replete with that same spontaneity: Out drunk in a boat, he fell into a river and drowned trying to embrace the moon.

Wandering Up Ample-Gauze Creek on a Spring Day

At the canyon's mouth, I'm singing. Soon
the path ends. People don't go any higher.

I scramble up cliffs into impossible valleys,
and follow the creek back toward its source.

Up where newborn clouds rise over open rock,
a guest come into wildflower confusions,

I'm still lingering on, my climb unfinished,
as the sun sinks away west of peaks galore.

Gazing at the Thatch-Hut Mountain Waterfall

I

Climbing west toward Incense-Burner Peak,
I look south and see a falls of water, a cascade

hanging there, three thousand feet high,
then seething dozens of miles down canyons.

Sudden as lightning breaking into flight,
its white rainbow of mystery appears. Afraid

at first the celestial Star River is falling,
splitting and dissolving into cloud heavens,

I look up into force churning in strength,
all power, the very workings of Change-Maker.

It keeps ocean winds blowing ceaselessly,
shines a mountain moon back into empty space,

empty space it tumbles and sprays through,
rinsing green cliffs clean on both sides,

sending pearls in flight scattering into mist
and whitewater seething down towering rock.

Here, after wandering among these renowned
mountains, the heart grows rich with idleness.

Why talk of cleansing elixirs of immortality?
Here, the world's dust rinsed from my face,

I'll stay close to what I've always loved,
content to leave that peopled world forever.

2

Sunlight on Incense-Burner kindles violet smoke.
Watching the distant falls hanging there, river

headwaters plummeting three thousand feet in flight,
I see the Star River falling through nine heavens.

On Yellow-Crane Tower, Farewell to Meng Hao-jan Who's Leaving for Yang-chou

From Yellow-Crane Tower, my old friend leaves the west.
Downstream to Yang-chou, late spring a haze of blossoms,

distant glints of lone sail vanish into emerald-green air:
nothing left but a river flowing on the borders of heaven.

At Golden-Ridge

Tucked into the earth, Golden-Ridge City,
the river curving past, flowing away:

there were once a million homes here,
and crimson towers along narrow lanes.

A vanished country all spring grasses
now, the palace buried in ancient hills,

this moon remains, facing the timeless
island across Hou Lake waters, empty.

Mountain Dialogue

You ask why I've settled in these emerald mountains:
I smile, mind of itself perfectly idle, and say nothing.

Peach blossoms drift streamwater away deep in mystery
here, another heaven and earth, nowhere people know.

Li Po (701–762)

Drinking Alone Beneath the Moon

Among the blossoms, a single jar of wine.
No one else here, I ladle it out myself.

Raising my cup, I toast the bright moon,
and facing my shadow makes friends three,

though moon has never understood wine,
and shadow only trails along behind me.

Kindred a moment with moon and shadow,
I've found a joy that must infuse spring:

I sing, and moon rocks back and forth;
I dance, and shadow tumbles into pieces.

Sober, we're together and happy. Drunk,
we scatter away into our own directions:

intimates forever, we'll wander carefree
and meet again in Star River distances.

Li Po (701–762)

On Peace-Anew Tower

On this tower as I leave our homeland,
late autumn wounds thoughts of return,

and heaven long, a setting sun far off,
this cold clear river keeps flowing away.

Chinese clouds rise from mountain forests;
Mongol geese on sandbars take flight.

A million miles azure pure— the eye
reaches beyond what ruins our lives.

Watching a White Falcon Set Loose

High in September's frontier winds, white
brocade feathers, the Mongol falcon flies

alone, a flake of snow, a hundred miles
some fleeting speck of autumn in its eyes.

Night Thoughts at East-Forest Monastery
on Thatch-Hut Mountain

Alone, searching for blue-lotus roofs,
I set out from city gates. Soon, frost

clear, East-Forest temple bells call out,
Tiger Creek's moon bright in pale water.

Heaven's fragrance everywhere pure
emptiness, heaven's music endless,

I sit silent. It's still, the entire Buddha-
realm in a hair's-breadth, mind-depths

all bottomless clarity, in which vast
kalpas begin and end out of nowhere.

Spur of the Moment

Facing wine, I missed night coming on
and falling blossoms filling my robes.

Drunk, I rise and wade the midstream moon,
birds soon gone, and people scarcer still.

Reverence-Pavilion Mountain, Sitting Alone

The birds have vanished into deep skies.
A last cloud drifts away, all idleness.

Inexhaustible, this mountain and I
gaze at each other, it alone remaining.

Autumn River Songs

5

Autumn River's white gibbons seem countless,
a dancing flurry of leaps, snowflakes flying:

Coaxing kids out of the branches, they descend,
and in a frolic, drink at the moon in water.

14

Smelter fires light up heaven and earth,
red stars swirling through purple smoke.

In the moonlit night, men's faces flushed,
worksong echoes out over the cold river.

17

Hardly ashore at Clear Creek, I hear it:
clarity, the voice of such perfect clarity.

At dusk, in farewell to a mountain monk,
I bow in deep reverence to white cloud.

Listening to a Monk's Ch'in Depths

Carrying a *ch'in* cased in green silk, a monk
descended from Eyebrow Mountain in the west.

When he plays, even in a few first notes,
I hear the pines of ten thousand valleys,

and streams rinse my wanderer's heart clean.
Echoes linger among temple frost-fall bells,

night coming unnoticed in emerald mountains,
autumn clouds banked up, gone dark and deep.

9/9, out drinking on Dragon Mountain

[handwritten: 9th day 9th Month Ever & Ever]

9/9, out drinking on Dragon Mountain,
I'm an exile among yellow blossoms smiling.

Soon drunk, I watch my cap tumble in wind,
dance in love— a guest the moon invites.

Li Po (701–762)

At Hsieh T'iao's House

The lingering Green Mountain sun has set.
It's all silence at Hsieh T'iao's home now:

sounds of people wandering bamboo gone,
the moon mirrored white in a pool empty.

Tattered grasses fill the deserted courtyard,
and green moss shrouds the forgotten well.

Nothing stirs but the idle clarity of breezes
playing midstream across water and stone.

Inscribed on a Wall at Summit-Top Temple

Staying the night at Summit-Top Temple,
you can reach out and touch the stars.

I venture no more than a low whisper,
afraid I'll startle the people of heaven.

Clear Creek Chant

It renders the mind clear— Clear Creek,
its water unrivaled for such pure color.

I can gaze into the bottom of its always
fresh repose. Is there anything like this

brilliant mirror in which people walk?
It's a wind-painting birds cross through,

and at nightfall, shrieking monkeys leave
all lament over distant wandering empty.

Looking for Yung, the Recluse Master

Emerald peaks polish heaven. I wander,
forgetting the years, sweep clouds away

in search of the ancient Way. Resting
against a tree, I listen to streamwater,

black ox dozing among warm blossoms,
white crane asleep in towering pines.

A voice calls through river-tinted dusk,
but I've descended into cool mist alone.

Li Po (701–762)

Thoughts in Night Quiet

Seeing moonlight here at my bed,
and thinking it's frost on the ground,

I look up, gaze at the mountain moon,
then back, dreaming of my old home.

Tu Fu (712–770)

The T'ang China of Tu Fu's earlier years is remembered as the pinnacle of Chinese civilization: the government was impeccable and the country at peace, the common people prospered, and the most dramatic cultural renaissance in Chinese history was under way. All of this ended in Tu Fu's 44th year, when a catastrophic civil war broke out, devastating the country and leaving two-thirds of the people either dead or cast adrift as homeless refugees. Tu Fu tried to do his share in the government's campaign to rescue the country, but after much frustration and little success, he resigned with the hope of establishing a reclusive life devoted to his art.

Tu succeeded spectacularly as an artist, becoming the greatest of China's poets, but his was not to be a settled life of tranquil dwelling far from human affairs. He never stopped agonizing over the social situation, which is a constant presence in his poems. And though the fighting had appeared to be nearly over when he resigned, it continued for years. Tu Fu did manage to settle his family several times, but they were always driven on by the incessant fighting that kept flaring up all around the country. So Tu's recluse life was spent wandering the outer fringes of the Chinese cultural sphere as a kind of itinerant recluse.

It was this exile wandering that provided Tu Fu with his unique perspective on rivers-and-mountains wilderness. Though he responded poetically at the level of immediate experience, Tu achieved a panoramic view of the human drama: he saw it as part of China's vast landscape of natural process, a vision distilled in one of the most famous lines in Chinese poetry: "The nation falls into ruins; rivers and mountains continue." Tu's work articulates exile in this world of rivers and mountains, but also the exile we all share in a wilderness cosmology of relentless transformation—for we are, like all things, just fleeting forms already on their way somewhere else. Poised between black despair and exquisite beauty, his was a geologic perspective, a vision of the human cast against the elemental sweep of the universe.

Gazing at the Sacred Peak

What's this ancestor Exalt Mountain like?
An unending green of north and south,

ethereal beauty Change-Maker distills
where *yin* and *yang* split dusk and dawn.

It breathes out banks of cloud. Birds clear
my eyes vanishing home. One day soon,

at the summit, all the other peaks will be
small enough to hold in a single glance.

Inscribed on the Wall at Chang's Recluse Home

In spring mountains, alone, I set out to find you.
Axe strokes crack— crack and quit. Silence doubles.

I pass snow and ice lingering along cold streams,
then, at Stone-Gate in late light, enter these woods.

You harm nothing: deer roam here each morning;
want nothing: auras gold and silver grace nights.

Facing you on a whim in bottomless dark, the way
here lost— I feel it drifting, this whole empty boat.

Tu Fu (712—770)

The New Moon

Thin slice of ascending light, arc tipped
aside all its bellied dark— the new moon

appears and, scarcely risen beyond ancient
frontier passes, edges behind clouds. Silver,

changeless— the Star River spreads across
empty mountains scoured with cold. White

dew dusts the courtyard, chrysanthemum
blossoms clotted there with swollen dark.

Leaving the City

It's frost-bitter cold, and late, and falling
dew muffles my gaze into bottomless skies.

Smoke trails out over distant salt mines,
snow-covered peaks angling shadows east.

Armies haunt my homeland still, and war
drums throb in this other place. A guest

here in this river city tonight, I return
again to shrieking crows, my old friends.

Tu Fu (712–770)

Brimmed Whole

A river moon only feet away, storm-lanterns
alight late in the second watch. . . . Serene

flock of fists on sand— egrets asleep when
a fish leaps in the boat's wake, shivering, cry.

Skies Clear at Dusk

Dusk's failing flare sends slant light deep.
Drifting clouds thin away— none return.

A rainbow upriver drinks at lit distances.
In the gorge, remnant rains scatter away

as ducks and cranes set out high overhead,
leaving bears to their well-fattened ease.

Autumn equinox. Still a wanderer, still here.
Dew on bamboo. Twilight gone spare, spare.

Reflections in Autumn

Jade-pure dew wounds maple forests, Shaman Mountain
forests rising from Shaman Gorge, *ch'i*-wind heaving.

The river's billows and waves breach skies churning.
Clouds drift above passes, touching darkness to earth.

Chrysanthemum blossoms have opened tears here twice:
my lost lives, my lone boat moored to a homesick heart. . . .

Everywhere, urgently, winter clothes are cut to pattern.
Fulling-stone rhythms fill the air, tightening at twilight.

Night at the Tower

Yin and *yang* cut brief autumn days short. Frost and snow
clear, leaving a cold night open at the edge of heaven.

Marking the fifth watch, grieving drums and horns erupt.
The Star River, shadows trembling, floats in Triple Gorge.

Pastoral weeping, war's sound now in how many homes,
and tribal songs drifting from woodcutters and fishermen. . . .

Slumber-Dragon, Leap-Stallion: all brown earth in the end.
And the story of our lives just opens away— vacant, silent.

Tu Fu (712–770)

Morning Rain

A slight rain comes, bathed in dawn light.
I hear it among treetop leaves before mist

arrives. Soon it sprinkles the earth and,
windblown, follows clouds away. Deepened

colors grace thatch homes for a moment.
Flocks and herds of things wild all glisten

faintly. Then, scent of musk opens across
half a mountain, and lingers on past noon.

The Musk Deer

Clear streams lost forever, you'll end
served up in jade dainties. Too little

talent for the life of hermit immortals,
unable even to resent fine kitchens—

once times fall apart, anything's a trifle,
faint voice at disaster's heart, anything.

Noblemen noble as thieves, gluttonous,
you'll get wolfed down in a royal trice.

Thatch House

Our thatch house perched where land ends,
we leave the brushwood gate always open.

Dragons and fish settle into evening waters.
Moon and stars drifting above autumn peaks,

dew gathers clarity, then thaws. High clouds
thin away— none return. Women man wind-

tossed boats anchored here: young, ashamed,
that river life battering their warm beauty.

Tu Fu (712—770)

8th Moon, 17th Night: Facing the Moon

The autumn moon rose full again tonight.
In this river village, a lone old wanderer

hoisting blinds, I return to its radiance.
As I struggle along with a cane, it follows,

and bright enough to rouse deep dragons,
it scatters roosting birds back and forth.

All around my thatch study, orange groves
shine: clear dew aching with fresh light.

Dawn Landscape

The last watch has sounded in K'uei-chou.
Color spreading above Solar-Terrace Mountain,

a cold sun clears high peaks. Clouds linger,
blotting out canyons below tangled ridges,

and deep Yangtze banks keep sails hidden.
Beneath clear skies: clatter of falling leaves.

And these deer at my bramble gate: so close
here, we touch our own kind in each other.

In Reply to a Letter from Meng, Who's Gone Searching for His Old Village

After all that loss and ruin, I live at peace
far from Lo-yang summits, still unraveling

this question cloud-hidden peaks all pose.
I never leave these thorn-bramble depths—

north winds yellow leaves tumbling away,
southern streams old-age laments. Ten years

a guest of lakes and rivers— this mind all
lingering dusk grows boundless, boundless.

Tu Fu (712–770)

Autumn Pastoral

Pastoral autumn ever more unearthly,
a cold river jostles azure space. My boat

tethered to Well-Rope, aboriginal star,
I sited my house in a southern village

waste. Workers pick ripe dates here,
but I hoe plots of sunflower wreckage

myself. And dinners, the food of old men
now, I share out midstream to the fish.

Facing Night

Outside a lone city, our river village rests
among confusions of tumbling streams.

Deep mountains hurry brief winter light
here. Tall trees calming bottomless wind,

cranes glide in to mist-silvered shallows,
and hens nestle into thatch roofs. Tonight,

lamplight scattered across *ch'in* and books
all night long, I can see through my death.

Tu Fu (712–770)

Night

I

Flutes mourn on the city wall. It is dusk:
the last birds cross our village graveyard,

and after decades of battle, their war-tax
taken, people return in deepening night.

Trees darken against cliffs. Leaves fall.
The river of stars faintly skirting beyond

frontier passes, I gaze at a tilting Dipper,
the moon thin, magpies done with flight.

2

A sliver of moon lulls through clear night.
Half abandoned to sleep, lampwicks char.

Deer wander, uneasy among howling peaks,
and forests of falling leaves startle cicadas.

I remember mince treats east of the river,
think of our boat adrift in falling snow. . . .

Tribal songs rise, rifling the stars. Here,
at the edge of heaven, I inhabit my absence.

Opposite a Post-Station, the Boat
Moonlit Beside a Monastery

My boat mirroring a clear, bright moon
deep in the night, I leave lanterns unlit:

a gold monastery beyond green maples,
a red post-tower here beside white water.

Faint, drifting from a city, a crow's cry
fades. Full of wild grace, egrets sleep.

Hair white, a guest of lakes and rivers,
I tie blinds open and sit alone, sleepless.

Wei Ying-wu (c. 737–792)

Like Hsieh Ling-yün, Wei Ying-wu was born into one of the wealthiest and most powerful families in the empire. But the family's fortunes were in decline, and when Wei was about twenty, the An Lu-shan rebellion ravaged the country, leaving China's cultural splendor and the Wei family in ruins. The loss of his aristocratic life was apparently a kind of awakening for Wei: he soon moved to Mind-Jewel Monastery, where he stayed for several years. This marked the beginning of a life centered in quiet contemplation and poetry. Like Wang Wei, he was by nature a recluse, but never left government service completely: he needed the salary to survive, and he had also become very concerned with the desperate plight of common people in an age of widespread poverty and devastation. He held a number of positions, both in the capital and in distant provinces. But it seems Wei was never really comfortable in these positions, even though some were quite important, and he generally ended up leaving them. He preferred the simplicity of a recluse life at a mountain monastery or farm, in spite of the relative poverty it sometimes entailed.

Wei Ying-wu's poetry is perhaps best known for the rivers-and-mountains poems he wrote later in life, during those periods of quiet reclusion. His poetry in this mode is especially revered for its calm and understated simplicity, as well as its clarity of description. But however secluded the world of these poems may be, they reflect his continued involvement with social issues. Wei lived in the ruins of what was perhaps China's greatest moment of cultural splendor, and his poems are often suffused with an ineffable sense of absence. Here lies the uneasy magic of Wei's quiet poems: in them, loss and absence often seem indistinguishable from the emptiness of enlightenment.

Climbing Above Mind-Jewel Monastery, Where
I Lived Long Ago

Incense terraces and kingfisher-green ridgelines tower into sky.
Misty trees and ten thousand homes fill the river's sunlit water.

The monks live nearby, but they would be such strangers by now.
I sit all stillness, listening to a faint bell record these lost years.

Fringes of Mist, a Bell

Where does it begin? All remote solitude,
all recluse distances bidding dusk farewell,

it follows thought's landscape far and wide,
scatters out and drifts thinning mist away.

Glimpsed in the still night of autumn wilds,
a lone mountain monk wanders back home.

Autumn Night, Sent to Ch'iu Tan

This autumn night become thoughts of you,
I wander along, offer cold heaven a chant.

In mountain emptiness, a pinecone falls.
My recluse friend must not be asleep either.

Outside My Office, Wandering in Moonlight

Outside the office, night such luminous depths,
the lovely moon's a delight wandering with me.

Descending across the river, it comes halfway
adrift on dew-tinged air, then suddenly startles

autumn, scattering color through open forests,
scrawling its disc on the current's utter clarity.

And reaching mind, it bestows boundless light
all silver-pure azure eluding us to perfection.

In the Depths of West Mountain, Visiting the Master

A disciple for years at Twin-Stream,
what brings you to these mountains?

Great luminaries keep the world at war,
but your mind flowing-water idleness,

you swept tigers from forests, and now
sit alone, utter stillness. Guarding this

frontier, we double silence, wander
narrow passes where clouds are born.

At West Creek in Ch'u-chou

Alone, I savor wildflowers tucked in along the creek,
and there's a yellow oriole singing in treetop depths.

Spring floods come rain-swollen and wild at twilight.
No one here at the ferry, a boat drifts across of itself.

Evening View

Already, at South Tower: evening stillness.
In the darkness, a few forest birds astir.

The bustling city-wall sinks out of sight—
deeper, deeper. Just four mountain peaks.

Sent to a Master of Way in the Utter-Peak Mountains

In my office library, the morning cold,
I suddenly think of a mountain guest

searching creeks for bramble kindling
and returning to cook white-stone soup.

I long to bring you a gourd full of wine,
soften endless nights of wind and rain,

but fallen leaves fill empty mountains:
all trace of your coming and going gone.

At Truth-Expanse Monastery, in the Dharma Master's West Library

At a thatch hut above riverside cliffs,
rapids far below: crystalline chimes

in vast rivers-and-mountains solitude.
Climbing into such views means pure

confusion. I straggled up First-Origin,
then followed Well-Creek Trail back to

temple trees hissing in endless winds,
this river lit with regret turning dark.

Entering the Carnelian Mountains Together

It's snowing on Stone-Gate Mountain. We leave no tracks.
Pine Valley's icy mists are thick with incense fragrance,

and in the courtyard, cold birds descend on scraps of food.
A tattered robe hangs in a tree. The old monk's gone now.

At Cloud-Wisdom Monastery, in the Ch'an Master's Courtyard

Exalted with age, you never leave here:
the gate-path is overgrown with grass.

But summer rains have come, bringing
fruits and herbs into such bright beauty,

so we stroll down into forests of shadow,
sharing what recluse birds feel at dusk,

freed even of our names. And this much
alone, we wander the countryside back.

Cold Mountain (Han Shan) (c. 7th–9th centuries)

Cold Mountain emptied out the distinction between Cold Mountain the poet and Cold Mountain the mountain. This is the essence of the Cold Mountain poems, so it is fitting that almost nothing is known about Cold Mountain the poet: he exists more as legend than historical fact. Legend has it that he lived alone on Cold Mountain, a summit in the Heaven-Terrace Mountains of southeast China, taking it as his namesake, and eventually his very identity. He often visited a nearby Ch'an monastery, where a like-minded friend in the kitchen shared leftovers with him, and the resident monks thought him quite insane. There are stories of his antics there, bantering with his friend and ridiculing the monks for their devout pursuit of an enlightenment they already possessed as part of their inherent nature. But mostly he roamed the mountains alone, a wild Ch'an sage writing poems on rocks and trees. These poems were collected by the local government prefect who, recognizing Cold Mountain's genius, assembled them into a collection that has been preserved. Over the centuries, these poems came to be widely admired in the literary and Ch'an communities of China. This admiration spread to Korea and Japan, and recently to the West: Gary Snyder's influential translations recreated Cold Mountain as a major contemporary American poet.

Cold Mountain is remembered as a Ch'an poet; but he is, like virtually all great Chinese poets, most fundamentally a Taoist poet. In fact, he is entirely in the mold of those wild sages that frequent the *Chuang Tzu*. He identifies the empty mind of Ch'an enlightenment with the mountain itself, but this is not the static mirroring of a timeless mountain realm: it is a deep Taoist dwelling within the cosmology, the dynamic spiritual ecology that mountain realm manifests so dramatically. According to the legend, Cold Mountain the poet was last seen when, slipping into a crevice that closed behind him, he vanished utterly into the mountain. Only poems remained, scrawled on rocks and trees: the record of a mountain working further and further into its own voice, its own singular language.

9

People ask about Cold Mountain Way.
Cold Mountain Road gives out where

confusions of ice outlast summer skies
and sun can't thin mists of blindness.

So how did someone like me get here?
My mind's just not the same as yours:

if that mind of yours were like mine,
you'd be right here in the midst of this.

28

If you're climbing Cold Mountain Way,
Cold Mountain Road grows inexhaustible:

long canyons opening across fields of talus,
broad creeks tumbling down mists of grass.

Moss is impossibly slick even without rain,
but this far up, pines need no wind to sing.

Who can leave the world's tangles behind
and sit with me among these white clouds?

67

The cold in these mountains is ferocious,
has been every year since the beginning.

Crowded peaks locked in perennial snows,
recluse-dark forests breathing out mists,

grasses never sprout before the solstice
and leaves start falling in early August.

This confusion includes a lost guest now,
searching, searching— no sky to be seen.

81

Springs flowing pure clarity in emerald streams,
moonlight's radiant white bathes Cold Mountain.

Leave wisdom dark: spirit's enlightened of itself.
Empty your gaze and this world's beyond silence.

I've lived out tens of thousands of years
on Cold Mountain. Given to the seasons,

I vanished among forests and cascades,
gazed into things so utterly themselves.

No one ventures up into all these cliffs
hidden forever in white mist and cloud.

It's just me, thin grass my sleeping mat
and azure heaven my comforting quilt:

happily pillowed on stone, I'm given to
heaven and earth changing on and on.

Under vast arrays of stars, dazzling depths of night,
I light a lone lamp among cliffs. The moon hasn't set.

It's the unpolished jewel. Incandescence round and full,
it hangs there in blackest-azure skies, my very mind.

The cloud road's choked with deep mist. No one gets here that way,
but these Heaven-Terrace Mountains have always been my home:

a place to vanish among five-thousand-foot cliffs and pinnacles,
ten thousand creeks and gorges all boulder towers and terraces.

I follow streams in birch-bark cap, wooden sandals, tattered robes,
and clutching a goosefoot walking-stick, circle back around peaks.

Once you realize this floating life is the perfect mirage of change,
it's breathtaking— this wild joy at wandering boundless and free.

220

Everyone who glimpses Cold Mountain
starts complaining about insane winds,

about a look human eyes can't endure
and a shape nothing but tattered robes.

They can't fathom these words of mine.
Theirs I won't even mention. I just tell

all those busy people bustling around:
come face Cold Mountain for a change.

I delight in the everyday Way, myself
among mist and vine, rock and cave,

wildlands feeling so boundlessly free,
white clouds companions in idleness.

Roads don't reach those human realms.
You only climb this high in no-mind:

I sit here on open rock: a lone night,
a full moon drifting up Cold Mountain.

282

Amid ten thousand streams up among
thousands of clouds, a man all idleness

wanders blue mountains all day long,
returns at night to sleep below cliffs.

In the whirl of springs and autumns,
to inhabit this calm, no tangles of dust:

it's sheer joy depending on nothing,
still as an autumn river's quiet water.

People taking Cold
Mountain Way never

arrive. Whoever does
is a tenfold Buddha.

Cicadas are singing,
raucous crows quiet.

Yellow leaves tumble.
White clouds sweep

across fields of talus,
peaks hidden deep.

Dwelling this alone,
I'm the perfect guide.

Look, look all around
here: any sign of me?

306

No one knows this
mountain I inhabit:

deep in white clouds,
forever empty, silent.

Cold Mountain (c. 7ᵗʰ–9ᵗʰ centuries)

309

Sage Cold Mountain
is forever like this:

dwells alone and free,
not alive, not dead.

Meng Chiao (751–814)

Until the age of forty, Meng Chiao lived as a poet-recluse associated with Ch'an poet-monks in south China. Meng left this life and went north, eventually settling as an impoverished poet in Lo-yang, the eastern capital. There, he became the founder of an experimental movement that defined the mid-T'ang as a unique period in Chinese poetry. Traditionally, Chinese poets thought of themselves as rendering immediate experience and their responses to it. But the mid-T'ang experimentalists reversed that equation: their focus was on imagining poems, and in so doing, creating new experience. That this approach, so dominant and taken for granted in Western poetry, would be considered experimental is eloquent testimony to the intense bond that connected the Chinese poet to the landscape of empirical reality. Leading the way for this mid-Tang experimental movement, Meng Chiao developed a new poetics of startling disorientations. It was a poetry of virtuosic beauty, and a poetry that anticipated landmark developments in the modern Western tradition by a millennium. Reflecting the T'ang Dynasty's catastrophic social situation, Meng's later work employed quasi-surreal and symbolist techniques, extending the dark extremities of Tu Fu's late work into a radically new poetry of bleak introspection.

There is a black side to the profound sense of dwelling that grounds Chinese culture, and Meng Chiao is perhaps its consummate poetic master. Our belonging to earth's natural processes has always been the primary source of spiritual affirmation in China's Taoist / Ch'an intellectual culture, but it also means belonging to the consuming forces that drive those processes. In an intellectual culture that found a meditative serenity in the emptiness of nonbeing, Meng was a dissenting voice. At its limits, as in "Laments of the Gorges," his quasi-surreal and symbolist techniques are capable of articulating nonbeing as a murderous furnace at the heart of change. But quite unlike his counterparts in our modern Western tradition, Meng Chiao employs these avant-garde techniques to explore the experience of being an integral part of the organic universe, and this sense of integration gives his fearful vision a kind of balance and deeper truth.

Laments of the Gorges

3

Triple Gorge one thread of heaven over
ten thousand cascading thongs of water,

slivers of sun and moon sheering away
above, and wild swells walled-in below,

splintered spirits glisten, a few glints
frozen how many hundred years in dark

gorges midday light never finds, gorges
hungry froth fills with peril. Rotting

coffins locked into tree roots, isolate
bones twist and sway, dangling free,

and grieving frost roosts in branches,
keeping lament's dark, distant harmony

fresh. Exile, tattered heart all scattered
away, you'll simmer in seething flame

here, your life like fine-spun thread,
its road a trace of string traveled away.

Offer tears to mourn the water-ghosts,
and water-ghosts take them, glimmering.

4

Young clear-voiced dragons in these
gorges howl. Fresh scales born of rock,

they spew froth of fetid rain, breath
heaving, churning up black sinkholes.

Strange new lights glint, and hungry
swords await. This venerable old maw

still hasn't eaten its fill. Ageless teeth
cry a fury of cliffs, cascades gnawing

through these three gorges, gorges
full of jostling and snarling, snarling.

Meng Chiao (751–814)

9

Water swords and spears raging in gorges,
boats drift across heaving thunder. Here

in the hands of these serpents and snakes,
you face everyday frenzies of wind and rain,

and how many fleeing exiles travel these
gorges, gorges rank inhabitants people?

You won't find a heart beneath this sheen,
this flood that's stored away aftermath

forever. Arid froth raising boundless mist,
froth all ablaze and snarling, snarling—

what of that thirst for wisdom when you're
suddenly here, dead center in these waters?

10

Death-owls call in human voices. Dragons
wolf down heaving mountain waters. Here

in broad daylight, with all the enticing
serenity of a clear and breezy sky, they

beggar wisdom, snarling everything alive
in fetid gatherings of vine-covered depths.

Want filling fanged cascades bottomless,
sawtooth froth swells everywhere. Nesting

birds can't settle in trees tilted so askew,
trees gibbons leaping and swinging fill.

Who can welcome laments of the gorges,
gorges saying *What will come will come.*

Autumn Thoughts

I

Lonely bones can't sleep nights. Singing
insects keep calling them, calling them.

And the old have no tears. When they sob,
autumn weeps dewdrops. Strength failing

all at once, as if cut loose, and ravages
everywhere, like weaving unraveled,

I touch thread-ends. No new feelings.
Memories crowding thickening sorrow,

how could I bear southbound sails, how
wander rivers and mountains of the past?

2

Under this autumn moon's face of frozen
beauty, the spirit driving an old wanderer

thins away. Cold dewdrops fall shattering
dreams. Biting winds comb cold through

bones. The sleeping-mat stamped with my
seal of sickness, whorled grief twisting,

there's nothing to depend on against fears.
Empty, sounds beginning nowhere, I listen.

Wu-t'ung trees, bare and majestic, sing
sound and echo clear as a *ch'in*'s lament.

5

Bamboo ticking in wind speaks. In dark
isolate rooms, I listen. Demons and gods

fill my frail ears, so blurred and faint I
can't tell them apart. Year-end leaves,

dry rain falling, scatter. Autumn clothes
thin cloud, my sick bones slice through

things clean. Though my bitter chant
still makes a poem, I'm withering autumn

ruin, strength following twilight away.
Trailed out, this fluttering thread of life:

no use saying it's tethered to the very
source of earth's life-bringing change.

Liu Tsung-yüan (773–819)

Liu Tsung-yüan came only grudgingly to wilderness. Liu devoted himself to the Confucian ideal of improving the lives of common people, working as a passionate reformer in the government. He enjoyed a meteoric rise through government ranks, culminating at the age of thirty-two when he was part of a small group of men who effectively controlled the government. This group introduced many radical reforms that common people applauded but reactionary factions of the aristocracy resented. Within a few months these factions staged a palace coup: the emperor was overthrown, and everyone in the reformist group was exiled.

Liu spent the rest of his life as an exile in the far south. He had written very little before his exile, for he was wholly occupied with what mattered most to him: political action. But in exile he turned to spiritual cultivation, and poetry played a major role in this new life. Like many from north China, Liu was enthralled with the beautiful landscapes he found in the south. He began wandering almost obsessively among them, and with this came naturally a serious commitment to the Taoist and Ch'an thought that gave rivers and mountains such depth in ancient China. He studied under several Ch'an masters, spending a good deal of time in monasteries. And the poetry that resulted from his spiritual cultivation of wilderness established Liu as one of the T'ang Dynasty's leading rivers-and-mountains poets. He also wrote essays that were at least as influential. In fact, he is sometimes credited with establishing the rivers-and-mountains essay as a significant genre in Chinese literature.

Getting Up Past Midnight and Gazing Across the West Garden, I Encounter the Rising Moon

Waking to the sound of heavy dew falling,
I open the door, gaze past the west garden

to a cold moon rising over eastern ridges,
scattered bamboo, roots gone clear, clear.

Distance clarifies a waterfall into silence.
Now and then, a mountain bird calls out.

I lean on a column, stay till dawn in these
isolate depths of quiet: no words, no words.

Aimless Wandering: First Ascent, West Mountain

I came in exile to this prefecture, and was full of constant worry and fear, so I often set out to wander free and easy, far and wide. Hiking away the days with friends, I climbed towering peaks and roamed deep forests. Together we exhausted winding canyons, recluse cascades and strange rocks— no distance too far. We spread mats in the grass, then sat tipping a winepot until we were drunk. Before long, we fell asleep pillowed on each other's bellies, and in dreams shared insights beyond the limits of thought. Eventually we woke and got to our feet, then started back. Among all the rivers and mountains of this prefecture, no wonder eluded us, or so I thought. But the strange and majestic West Mountain was still unknown to me.

On the 28th sun of this year's 9th moon, sitting in the West Pavilion of Dharma-Splendor Monastery, I looked out at West Mountain and suddenly realized how wondrous it is. I called a few servants together, then everyone crossed the Hsiang River and started up along Deep-Dye Stream. Soon we were hacking a trail through thickets of briar and thornwood, burning the cut brush as we went. We kept on all the way up to summit rocks, where we scrambled up the final pitch clinging to vines. Then at last we sat down, legs spread, and let our eyes ramble in delight.

There were three or four prefectures spread out below our mats: vistas rising and falling, mountain expanses and deep lakes, all looking like little anthills and hollows. A few inches were a thousand miles crumpled together and heaped up. Nothing was hidden from sight. White clouds all around in blue skies stretching past the edge of heaven: a single view filled all four directions. And so I began to understand how majestic that mountain is, nothing like common hills. I felt myself mingling away everywhere into luminous *ch'i*, vast and distant and never reaching its limits. I wandered with the Maker-of-Things, boundless-deep and swelling and never fathoming its inexhaustible extent.

We poured cups full of wine, and soon drunk didn't notice the sun set. Twilight's azure dark came out of the distance, and before long we couldn't see a thing. But I still wasn't ready to start back. Mind motion-less and body set adrift, I found myself shading into the ten thousand changes, and realized that I'd never even begun to wander, that my wandering was just then beginning.

River Snow

A thousand peaks: no more birds in flight.
Ten thousand paths: all trace of people gone.

In a lone boat, rain cloak and hat of reeds,
an old man's fishing the cold river snow.

Returning to Compass-Line Cliff's Waterfall, I Stay Overnight Below the Cliffwall

All spring longing for this distant realm
makes it pure joy to see. This time, lavish

midsummer forests so rich with shadow,
it's like looking into dark-enigma gardens.

Dangling ice glints, dazzling sunlit mist,
and thunderstorms startle broad daylight,

windsong fills reeds along the shallows
where cranes dance deep among clouds,

and green limbs of ancient moss freeze,
dusky grass kingfisher feathers awash.

Brilliant silvers ranged across emptiness,
restless waves swell, gathering cold light,

and around this lit abyss of sunken pearl,
shoreline waist-jewels tinkle, bells clitter.

Above recluse cliffs like painted screens,
a new moon, jade-white arc in cold night,

rises. Stars fill the river. It almost seems
I'll fall asleep in the magic of home here.

Before Crossing the Ridges

All learning overturned in your pond's ink-dark ripples,
your tree of life scattering its branches: it's breathtaking.

Just one darling girl left now. She plays in courtyard dirt,
empty mind fluent in all those scribbled sparrow tracks.

An Old Fisherman

An old fisherman passes the night below western cliffs,
draws clear Hsiang water, lights a fire of Ch'u bamboo.

Mist clears. Sun rises. No one in sight. Just one sound,
one paddle-stroke among rivers-and-mountains green.

And looking away, it's all horizon touching midstream,
no-mind clouds chasing each other across the clifftops.

In Reply to Chia P'eng of the Mountains, Sent Upon Seeing That the Pine He Planted Outside My Office Has Begun to Prosper

Flourish and ruin keep leaving each other,
but no-mind stays, dark-enigma's fruition.

The bloom of youth scatters steadily away
and grandeur crumbles to its tranquil end,

but mountain streams continue here in this
green pine you brought to this courtyard,

deep snows showing off its radiant beauty
and cold blossoms its kingfisher-greens.

At dawn, even a pure recluse must yearn:
now, I just invite clear wind for company.

Gazing at Mountains with Ch'an Monk Primal-Expanse: Sent to Loved Ones Home in the Capital

Everywhere here: jagged coastal mountains, sword-tip sharp,
and now autumn's come, every one slices my grief-torn heart.

Dying into change, into thousands and hundreds of thousands,
I'll scatter onto every peak and gaze, gaze on away homeward.

Po Chü-i (772–846)

The Chinese poetic tradition consistently valued clarity and depth of wisdom, rather than mere complexity and virtuosity. In this, Po Chü-i is the quintessential Chinese poet. He was a devoted student of Ch'an Buddhism, and it was Ch'an that gave much of the clarity and depth to his life and work. This is immediately apparent in his voice and subject matter, but Ch'an is perhaps more fundamentally felt in the poetics shaping Po's poetry. In Ch'an practice, the self and its constructions of the world dissolve away until nothing remains but empty mind—empty mind mirroring the world, leaving its ten thousand things utterly simple, utterly themselves, and utterly sufficient. This suggests one possible Ch'an poetry: an egoless poetry such as Wang Wei's. But there is another possibility for Ch'an poetry: the poetry of an egoless ego.

The quiet response of even the most reticent poem is still a construction. Po knew this well, but it seems he came to realize that the self is also one of those ten thousand things that are utterly themselves and sufficient. Taoist thought would describe this insight rather differently, as the understanding that self is always already selfless: it is but a momentary form among the constant transformation of earth's ten thousand things, and so is, most fundamentally, the emptiness of nonbeing, that source which endures through all change. This insight results in a poetry quite different from Wang Wei's. Rather than Wang Wei's strategy of emptying the self among the ten thousand things, this poetics opens the poem to the various movements of self, weaving it into the fabric of the ten thousand things, and Po Chü-i was a master of its subtle ways. As such, he initiated a major strand in Chinese poetic thinking: an "interiorization of wilderness" that came to be the most distinctive trait of Sung Dynasty poetry.

In a culture that made no fundamental distinction between heart and mind (see Key Terms: *hsin*), Po Chü-i inhabited everyday experience at a level where a simple heart is a full heart and a simple mind is an empty mind. Such is his gentle power: the sense in his poems of dwelling at the very center of one's life, combining the intimacies of a full heart and the distances of an empty mind.

Hsiang-yang Travels: Thinking of Meng Hao-jan

Emerald Ch'u mountain peaks and cliffs,
emerald Han River flowing full and fast:

Meng's writing survives here, its elegant
ch'i now facets of changing landscape.

But today, chanting the poems he left us
and thinking of him, I find his village

clear wind, all memory of him vanished.
Dusk light fading, Hsiang-yang empty,

I look south to Deer-Gate Mountain, haze
lavish, as if some fragrance remained,

but his old mountain home is lost there:
mist thick and forests all silvered azure.

Autumn Thoughts, Sent Far Away

We share all these disappointments of failing
autumn a thousand miles apart. This is where

autumn wind easily plunders courtyard trees,
but the sorrows of distance never scatter away.

Swallow shadows shake out homeward wings.
Orchid scents thin, drifting from old thickets.

These lovely seasons and fragrant years falling
lonely away— we share such emptiness here.

Po Chü-i (772–846)

Ch'in *Song in Clear Night*

The moon's risen. Birds have settled in.
Now, sitting in these empty woods, silent

mind sounding the borders of idleness,
I can tune the *ch'in*'s utter simplicities:

from the wood's nature, a cold clarity,
from a person's mind, a blank repose.

When mind's gathered clear calm *ch'i*,
wood can make such sudden song of it,

and after lingering echoes die away,
song fading into depths of autumn night,

you suddenly hear the source of change,
all heaven and earth such depths of clarity.

Po Chü-i (772–846)

Village Night

Frost-covered grass silvered azure, insect song tightens.
No one north of the village, no one south of the village,

I wander out the front gate and gaze across open fields.
Moonlight shimmers, turning wheat blossoms into snow.

Inscribed on a Wall at Jade-Spring Monastery

In the jade spring's clear green depths,
this body's far far off, a drifting cloud,

and a mind all idleness faces still water,
both perfect clarity, no trace of dust.

The gnarled bamboo staff's in a hand,
the silk cap on a head. Come on a whim

and gone down the mountain, the whim
vanished: can anyone know who I was?

My Thatch Hut Newly Built Below
Incense-Burner Peak, I Chant My Thoughts,
Then Copy Them Onto the Rocks

Facing Incense-Burner's north slope,
just west of Love-Bequeath Monastery,

majestic rock towers, stately and white,
where a clear stream tumbles and flows,

where dozens of austere pines abide
and supple bamboo a thousand strong.

Pines kingfisher-green canopies spread,
bamboo hung with flakes of green jade:

they've harbored no human dwelling
for who knows how many long years,

just gatherings of gibbons and birds
and mist adrift on empty wind all day.

An adept sunk in such karma delusion,
I came here one day, a Po named Chü-i,

a man whose entire life seemed wrong,
and seeing it all, feeling mind settle

into a place that could nurture old age,
I knew at once that I would never leave,

so I framed thatch eaves against cliffs
and cleared a ravine for tea gardens.

To keep ears rinsed clean, a waterfall
washes across the roof and into flight,

and for eyes pure and clear, water lilies
drift white below a stonework terrace.

Nestling a jar of wine in my left hand
and a *ch'in*'s five strings in my right,

I admire how easily contentment comes
just sitting here in the midst of all this,

and marveling at the song of heaven,
I blend in a few tipsy words and let it

voice my nature: a far-country recluse
caught in nets of human consequence.

My best years offered up day by day,
I trust old age to this mountain return,

a tired bird finding its thick forests,
a worn-out fish back in clear streams.

If I ever left here, where would I go—
that peopled realm all trial and peril?

My Thatched Mountain Hut Just Finished, Ch'i-Sited Below Incense-Burner Peak, I Write This on the East Wall

Three rooms and five spans— my new thatch hut boasts
stone stairs, cassia pillars and a bamboo-weave fence,

eaves lofty on the south to welcome warm winter sun,
doors and windows on the north for cool summer winds.

A waterfall sprinkling stonework dissolves into mist,
and bamboo brushing the windows grow lazy and wild.

Next spring, I'll get a side-room ready here on the east:
paper screens and cane blinds for my wife, my treasure.

In the Mountains, Asking the Moon

It's the same Ch'ang-an moon when I ask
which doctrine remains with us always.

It flew with me when I fled those streets,
and now shines clear in these mountains,

carrying me through autumn desolations,
waiting as I sleep away long slow nights.

If I return to my old homeland one day,
it will welcome me like family. And here,

it's a friend for strolling beneath pines
or sitting together on canyon ridgetops.

A thousand cliffs, ten thousand canyons—
it's with me everywhere, abiding always.

Enjoying Pine and Bamboo

I treasure what front eaves face
and all that north windows frame.

Bamboo winds lavish out windows,
pine colors exquisite beyond eaves,

I gather it all into isolate mystery,
thoughts fading into their source.

Others may feel nothing in all this,
but it's perfectly open to me now:

such kindred natures need share
neither root nor form nor gesture.

Po Chü-i (772—846)

Li the Mountain Recluse Stays
the Night on Our Boat

It's dusk, my boat such tranquil silence,
mist rising over waters deep and still,

and to welcome a guest for the night,
there's evening wine, an autumn *ch'in*.

A master at the gate of Way, my visitor
arrives from exalted mountain peaks,

lofty cloudswept face raised all delight,
heart all sage clarity spacious and free.

Our thoughts begin where words end.
Refining dark-enigma depths, we gaze

quiet mystery into each other and smile,
sharing the mind that's forgotten mind.

Off-Hand Chant

All the clothes and food I'll need here before me,
a mind free of all happiness, free of all sadness:

it's like some kind of afterlife. So what do you do
when you want nothing from this human world?

Eyes closed, I read classics of Way in silent depths,
and this idle, I hardly bow greeting Ch'an guests.

Luckily residue remains: a cloud-and-stream joy.
Every year I wander Dragon-Gate hills a few times.

Po Chü-i (772–846)

The West Wind

The west wind just began a few days ago,
and already the first leaves have flown.

Skies clearing anew, I don slight clogs
and clothes thick against this first chill,

channels rinsing thin water slowly away,
sparse bamboo a last trickle of slant light.

Soon, in a lane of green moss, dusk spare,
our houseboy comes leading cranes home.

After Quiet Joys at South Garden, *Sent By P'ei Tu*

This hut isolate and clear beside the pond:
surely this is what lofty thoughts must be,

blinds in the occasional breeze stirring,
a bridge shining late sun back into water.

I've grown quiet here, company to cranes,
and so idle I'm like any other cloud adrift.

Why bother to go study under Duke Liu
or search wild peaks for Master Red Pine?

Waves Sifting Sand

I

One anchorage of sand appears as another dissolves away,
and one fold of wave ends as another rises. Wave and sand

mingling together day after day, sifting through each other
without cease: they level up mountains and seas in no time.

2

White waves swell through wide open seas, boundless and beyond,
and level sands stretch into the four directions all endless depths:

evenings they dissolve and mornings reappear, sifting ever away,
their seasons transforming eastern seas into a field of mulberries.

3

Ten thousand miles across a lake where the grass never fades,
a lone traveler, you find yourself in rain among yellow plums,

gazing grief-stricken toward an anchorage of sand. Dark waves
wind keeps churned up: the sound of them slapping at the boat.

5

A day will no doubt come when dust flies at the bottom of seas,
and how can mountaintops avoid the transformation to gravel?

Young lovers may part, a man leaving, setting out on some boat,
but who could say they'll never come together again one day?

The North Window: Bamboo and Rock

A magisterial rock windswept and pure
and a few bamboo so lavish and green:

facing me, they seem full of sincerity.
I gaze into them and can't get enough,

and there's more at the north window
and along the path beside West Pond:

wind sowing bamboo clarities aplenty,
rain gracing the subtle greens of moss.

My wife's still here, frail and old as me,
but no one else: the children are gone.

Leave the window open. If you close it,
who'll keep us company for the night?

Climbing Mountains in Dream

Nights hiking Sung Mountain in dream,
just a goosefoot walking-stick and me:

a thousand cliffs, ten thousand canyons,
I wander until I've explored them all,

my stride in dream as it was in youth,
strong and sure and so free of disease.

When I wake, spirit become itself again
and body returned to flesh and blood,

I realize that in terms of body and spirit,
body grows sick while spirit's immune,

and yet body and spirit are both mirage,
dream and waking merest appearance.

Scarcely able to hobble around by day
then roaming free all night with ease:

in the equal division of day and night
what could I gain here, and what lose?

Chia Tao (779–843)

Chia Tao was for many years a Ch'an monk living in mountain monasteries. Although his poems make clear that he remained intimate with that community of mountain recluses, Chia eventually left that life, becoming an impoverished poet who devoted himself to poetry as a kind of spiritual discipline. He became a prominent member of the mid-T'ang experimental movement led by the elder Meng Chiao, trying his hand at their startling poetic effects. He eventually resumed a more mainstream commitment to immediate experience, although the experimental spirit continued to inform his poems. Indeed, it is that spirit which gives his poems their singular beauty.

The mid-T'ang experimental poets had turned away from Chinese poetry's traditional emphasis on rendering immediate experience, replacing it with a poetry of the imagination that strives to create new experience. Although he had left their excesses behind, Chia Tao continued their basic approach, but used it to create a new intimacy with *tzu-jan*. The quasi-surreal techniques typical of Meng Chiao and others in that group do appear in Chia Tao's work, though they are used sparingly and their purpose is not to shock readers. Instead, Chia Tao used them in subtle and self-effacing ways to chisel new depths of clarity in immediate experience. But it is in the overall texture of his poems that Chia's experimental spirit is most evident.

While virtually all of his major poems involve a remote rivers-and-mountains realm, Chia Tao developed and practiced his unique Way of poetry after leaving the mountains to live in the capital of Ch'ang-an, a very cosmopolitan city of two million people. Chia became legendary for wandering the city lost in imaginative reverie as he tried to hone a perfectly turned phrase or image. This was indicative of his experimental approach: he was not working to render his experience, but to create a distillation that was somehow more penetrating than actual experience could be. As a result, his poems present an almost too perfect rivers-and-mountains realm, as he tried to render the dimensions of Ch'an insight: clarity and simplicity, silence and open emptiness. And Chia's poetic method also reflects the Ch'an practice that had so deeply influenced him: to open these spiritual depths in the experience of wilderness, his poems operate by means of immediate knowing, startling images and juxtapositions, rather than intellectual statement. Chia Tao's Way of poetry proved extremely influential. It defined the "Late T'ang" style, becoming the dominant mode in rivers-and-mountains poetry for a century and a half after his death.

Sent to a Master of Silence on
White-Tower Mountain

Knowing you've returned to White-Tower,
I gaze into mountain distances, late skies

clearing. Mind tranquil in a stone house,
moon-shadow lingers across frozen lakes.

Thin cloud feathers into scraps and away.
Ancient trees fall and dry into firewood.

Past midnight, who hears stone chimes?
The cragged summit on West Peak is cold.

Chia Tao (779–843)

Looking for a Recluse I Can't Find

Asked beneath pines, a houseboy says
The master's gone off to gather herbs.

He's somewhere in these mountains
all depths of cloud who knows where.

Evening Landscape, Clearing Snow

Walking-stick in hand, I watch snow clear.
Ten thousand clouds and streams banked up,

woodcutters return to their simple homes,
and soon a cold sun sets among risky peaks.

A wildfire burns among ridgeline grasses.
Scraps of mist rise, born of rock and pine.

On the road back to a mountain monastery,
I hear it struck: that bell of evening skies!

A Sick Cicada

Flight impossible, a sick cicada
comes crawling up into my hand,

broken wings still thin crystal,
bitter call still clarity perfected.

Your belly blossoms dewdrop ice
and flecks of dust clot your eyes:

you're in a bad way. And hungry
orioles and kites intend the worst.

Mourning Meng Chiao

Orchids have lost their fragrance. Cranes no longer call.
Mourning has faded into autumn skies, and the moon's

brilliance gone dark. Ever since Master Meng Chiao died,
I've wandered my grief away in cloud-swept mountains.

South Lake

A light rain ends in isolate silence, where
woodland banks cradle a crystalline stream.

Peaks tipping into frontiers enter my boat.
Rice fields open cascades clear to the village.

Sounds of autumn lean toward forest colors,
and there's moon-shadow among cattail roots.

It's impossible, just lingering at anchor here.
Other nights call my spirit through dreams.

Early Autumn, Sent to be Inscribed on the Wall at Spirit-Refuge Monastery on India Mountain

A monastery nestled into peaks all early autumn:
on a cragged summit, it looks out across Wu-chou.

Deep in meditation, monks listen to cricket song,
and where nesting cranes were, monkeys frolic.

A mountain bell calls across empty river at dusk.
A shoreline moon, cold, rises over an old tower.

Mind unfurls its broad sails, but I'm still not here
in this place Hsieh Ling-yün long ago wandered.

For Li Chin-chou

Before and after Ch'i Li's recluse shrine,
mountain roads wander into white clouds.

Great pennants and flags come upstream,
then armies climb riverbanks into view,

dawn horns calling into people's dreams.
Autumn wind furling geese up into flight,

fog thins away. And sunlit dew everywhere,
the Han's riverbed gravel stands out clear.

Sitting at Night

Crickets ever more plentiful, autumn's far from shallow,
and now that the moon has sunk away, night grows deep.

It's the third watch, and branches of snow streak my hair.
Two peaks in a single thought: mind of the four patriarchs.

Tu Mu (803–853)

Of the many rivers-and-mountains poets who worked under the influence of Chia Tao's alternative aesthetic, only Tu Mu differentiated himself as a singular and major poet. Tu Mu was born into a very wealthy and illustrious family, his grandfather being the prime minister, but the family fortunes soon declined precipitously, and he spent much of his youth in relative poverty. In spite of this hardship, he somehow managed to acquire the erudition required for a career as a government officer. Tu's life-long career in government was not punctuated by periods of exile or retirement, as was common for the poets of ancient China. Instead, his intimacy with wild landscapes resulted from the stream of short-term positions he held: they were often in distant provinces, so he traveled and inhabited many of China's most striking landscapes.

Tu Mu's rivers-and-mountains poems are short, rarely more than eight lines, and his quatrains are especially renowned for the clarity and concision that so perfectly reflect his poetic Way. Clearly influenced by a deep familiarity with Ch'an practice, Tu cultivates the enigmas of history, landscape, and natural process in the very texture of his poems, which often feel like tiny collages of images: each fact or event perfectly apparent and perfectly itself. And in rendering these clarities as they are experienced by a mirror-like mind, he opens the fundamental human enigmas of consciousness and perception, revealing their organic relationship to the rivers-and-mountains realm.

Egrets

Robes of snow, crests of snow, and beaks of azure jade,
they fish in shadowy streams. Then startling up into

flight, they leave emerald mountains for lit distances.
Pear blossoms, a tree-full, tumble in the evening wind.

Anchored on Ch'in-huai River

Mist mantling cold waters, and moonlight shoreline sand,
we anchor overnight near a wine-house entertaining guests.

A nation lost in ruins: knowing nothing of that grief, girls
sing *Courtyard Blossoms.* Their voices drift across the river.

The Han River

Rich and full, all surging swells and white gulls in flight,
it flows springtime deep, its green a crystalline dye for robes.

Going south and coming back north, you grow older, older.
Late light lingers, farewell to a fishing boat bound for home.

Tu Mu (803–853)

A Mountain Walk

Climbing far into cold mountains, the stone path steepens.
White clouds are born up here, and there are houses too.

I stop to sit for awhile, savoring maple forests in late light:
frost-glazed leaves glistening red as mid-spring blossoms.

Unsent

Distant clouds, trees deep into mist,
autumn bathed in a river's clarity.

Where is she tonight, so beautiful?
Moonlight floods the mountaintops.

Spring South of the Yangtze

A thousand miles of oriole song, reds setting greens ablaze,
river villages with mountains for walls, wineshop flags, wind.

Of those four-hundred-eighty Southern Dynasty monasteries,
how many towers and terraces remain in this mist and rain?

Inscribed on Recluse Yüan's Lofty Pavilion

Water joins West River to sounds beyond heaven.
Outside the study, pine shadow sweeps clouds flat.

Who taught me to play this long flute? Together
we take to spring wind and frolic with moonlight.

Tu Mu (803–853)

Pond in a Bowl

Breach cut in green-moss earth,
it steals a distant flake of heaven.

White clouds emerge in mirror;
fallen moon shines below stairs.

Climbing Joy-Abroad Plateau

A lone bird vanishes in the endless sky's empty tranquillity.
And all boundless antiquity right here: it's disappearing too:

you can see it— the Han, dynasty of unrivaled achievement,
now just five imperial tombs, treeless, autumn winds rising.

A Clear Stream in Ch'ih-chou

I've played all day in the stream. Now twilight's yellow
lights autumn's destined coming, root of this white hair.

What is it I've trusted you to rinse a thousand times away,
until now, the dust fouling my brush-tip leaves no trace?

Sung Dynasty

(960–1279)

Mei Yao-ch'en (1002–1060)

Seen from the usual perspective of subject matter, Mei Yao-ch'en is not a particularly significant rivers-and-mountains poet. Mei was skeptical of the exquisite rivers-and-mountains poetry of Chia Tao and his followers in the fallow centuries of the late T'ang and early Sung Dynasties, skeptical of both its exquisite settings and its lofty spiritual aspirations. Mei's commitment was to reality in all its stuttering imperfections, so his poems often focused on precise physical description and attention to the most ordinary, even unsavory aspects of everyday life. He felt no need to poeticize what we call reality and the Chinese called *tzu-jan*, no need to extract lessons or sage wisdom from it. At the same time, Mei wrote with a kind of calm artlessness, which he considered the essence and most fundamental value of poetry. Mei's artlessness, central to a revitalization that made the Sung Dynasty the second great age of Chinese poetry, renewed and deepened the interiorization of wilderness begun by Po Chü-i two centuries earlier. This interiorization meant that Mei's most interesting and innovative rivers-and-mountains poems have nothing to do with rivers and mountains, for they offer an alternative, and perhaps finally more profound, engagement with *tzu-jan*.

Sage belonging to Lao Tzu's wilderness cosmology had typically been embodied in the subject matter of the poem, in the poem's explicit statement. But beginning with Mei Yao-ch'en, the major Sung poets *enact* that belonging in the form of the poem, rather than simply *portray* it in the poem's subject matter. Such poems have an easygoing, even bland feel. Profoundly influenced by their devoted Ch'an practice, Sung poets had seen through the need to assert a powerful individuality by shaping a singular vision of the world, for such an assertion isolates the individual outside of natural process. So Sung poetry traded the singular poetries typical of the T'ang Dynasty for a plain-spoken, uncrafted simplicity. But this simplicity of voice is actually quite complex: it is the selfless voice of wilderness in its human dimension; or at a deeper, more philosophical level, it is the poet participating in the original undifferentiated unity of nonbeing and in the indifferent process of *tzu-jan*'s unfolding. And rather than subsuming *tzu-jan*'s ten thousand things within a poetic vision, this unassuming simplicity allows them to stand out in their own self-sufficient singularity—a trait manifest in the Sung's commitment to realism, that detailed attention to things-at-hand, whatever they may be. The Sung revitalization represents a return to beginnings, to the lazybones insight of T'ao Ch'ien. And as with T'ao Ch'ien, however unassuming this poetic Way may appear, it reflects a deep wisdom that comes only after long cultivation.

East River

Reaching East River, I gaze across the water,
then sit facing a lone island. Boats creep forth.

Wild ducks, thoughts idle, sleep along the bank,
and in ancient trees, every limb is blossoming.

Pebble shorelines perfectly smooth, sieve-pure,
reed thickets bloom short and scissor-smooth.

So much to feel, but I can't stay. Night's come,
and my horse turning homeward— it's exhausted.

Mei Yao-ch'en (1002–1060)

8th Moon, 9th Sun: Getting Up in the Morning, I Go Out to the Latrine and Find Crows Feeding on Maggots There

Crows flapping around before sunup,
no telling which are male or female:

rat-carcass meals must be rare indeed
for them to come peck at shit-worms.

Soon stuffed, they rise into treetops,
cock their heads, cry into west wind.

I'm done listening to your evil omens.
Your feathers must reek with stench,

and divinities keep clean if they can
see into the origin and end of things.

On a Farewell Journey for Shih-hou, Who's Returning Home to Nan-yang, We Encounter a Vast Windstorm, So We Spend the Night at Solar-Heights Mountain Monastery, Then Continue On the Next Morning to Chiang Inn

Long ago I traveled out to send you off in spring wind,
spring wind a lavish delight, apricots in radiant bloom,

and now we share a farewell journey in autumn wind,
autumn wind clattering leaves down, rivers full of sand.

Frost knots our horses' fur, their manes buffeted out.
The servants shuffle along, scowls set against the cold,

and our rag coats blow open, cold cutting bone-deep
among dead trees scraping together, threatening fire.

Suddenly, from a cliff's belly, an old monastery appears,
and we dismount at last, happy to stay the night among

temples and halls terraced up and down the mountain,
majestic pine and cedar towering into ridgeline clouds.

As fallen leaves sweep swirling down long hallways
and curtains shaken clean beat in the abbot's window,

a terra-cotta mother-goddess nurses nine sweet babies,
hugging and caressing them, charming them with play:

it carries this distant traveler's thoughts back to family,
makes me burn with longing to see my little ones again.

We huddle around a brazier as twilight sky turns black,
then borrow monk beds and sleep lit by shrine lamps,

but even under quilts aplenty, we're soon cold as iron.
It's nothing like home, though I can't afford blankets,

and soon awake, we wait out dawn, pillowed on arms
as our legs turn numb with cold, muscles cramped tight.

Mei Yao-ch'en (1002–1060)

Finally clappers ring out: wooden fish marking dawn.
And rising, we watch the Pleiades and Hyades arc west

as the wind's howl dies away and the east brightens.
Our doubtful servants pack, and we're about to set out,

when an old monk comes carrying inkstone and brush,
sweeps a wall clean, and asks me to write out the year.

After leaving the gates, we travel to a mountain inn,
its thatch roof blown off. It's just beams and rafters,

but we stay. Opening Mongol chairs, we laugh and talk,
and though you've given up wine, we spread our mats.

Hardly five-hundred miles left on your journey home,
and surely you have a purse of coins in your satchel,

but you shake out robes, eager to go while there's sun,
and no wonder: a devoted mother is waiting anxiously.

I, on the other hand, leave for vistas of rivers and seas,
thoughts haunted even there by these places we shared.

Farmers

Towering trees shade a brushwood gate,
emerald moss dappled with falling light.

They hoe lotus, a mountain moon rising,
and then, searching thin mist for a trail,

the old man leads a child, eyes following
their starveling ox taking its calf home.

And for dinner, back home in lamplight,
they savor white garlic pan-fried in dew.

Lunar Eclipse

A maid comes running into the house
talking about things beyond belief,

about the sky all turned to blue glass,
the moon to a crystal of black quartz.

It rose a full ten parts round tonight,
but now it's just a bare sliver of light.

My wife hurries off to fry roundcakes,
and my son starts banging on mirrors:

it's awfully shallow thinking, I know,
but that urge to restore is beautiful.

The night deepens. The moon emerges,
then goes on shepherding stars west.

Wang An-shih (1021–1086)

Wang An-shih was a remarkable figure: not only one of the great Sung Dynasty poets, but also the preeminent statesman of his time. The deep commitment felt by intellectuals in ancient China to both the Confucian realm of social responsibility and the Taoist realm of spiritual self-cultivation gave rise to a recluse ideal that answered both of these commitments. In the most mythic version of this ideal, a sage recluse living contentedly in the mountains recognizes that the nation is in crisis and needs his wisdom—so he reluctantly joins the government; resolves the crisis; and then, having no interest in the wealth and renown associated with that life, returns to cultivate his simple life of spiritual depth in the mountains. This ideal was enacted by countless intellectuals in ancient China, though in a bit more realistic form. They devoted themselves to public service, always watching for a chance to spend time in mountain seclusion (often at monasteries), and then at some point retired permanently from government service to live as recluses. Wang An-shih was one of the great exemplars of this recluse ideal. A devoted civil servant, frugal almost to a fault and completely immune, even hostile, to the grandeur of that life, Wang rose to no less a rank than prime minister. As prime minister, he instituted a controversial system of widespread social reforms in an effort to dramatically improve the lives of common people. And once these reforms were in place, he retired to a reclusive life in the countryside near Chiang-ning, on the south shore of the Yangtze River.

Wang spent his later years practicing Ch'an with great devotion; wandering the mountains around his home, a passion that was an extension of his Ch'an cultivation of no-mind; and writing poems that reflected his Taoist / Ch'an cultivation of the rivers-and-mountains realm. In dramatic contrast to his majestic stature as the most powerful statesman in China, Wang's reputation as one of the Sung Dynasty's greatest poets is based on the short, unassuming rivers-and-mountains poems he wrote after retiring, most notably quatrains. The quatrain form was perfect for the Sung's poetics of selfless artlessness, and the fact that a man of such majestic stature would focus on it is an indication of the grandeur inherent in that unassuming simplicity of voice. In these poems, Wang transforms Mei Yao-ch'en's poetics of artlessness into a form of Ch'an no-mind, and combines it with Chia Tao's Late T'ang rivers-and-mountains tradition. This combination made Wang the originary rivers-and-mountains poet in the Sung tradition.

Wandering on Bushel Mountain

Gazing all day into mountains, I can't get enough of mountains.
Retire into mountains, and mountains become your old masters:

when mountain blossoms scatter away, mountains always remain,
and in empty mountain streamwater, mountains deepen idleness.

Middle years

Middle years devoted to the nation, you live a fleeting dream,
and home again in old age, you wander borderland wilderness.

Looking south to green mountains, it's clear I'm not so isolated:
here on Five Lakes in spring, they come aboard my little boat.

Wang An-shih (1021–1086)

Above the Yangtze

North of the Yangtze, autumn shadow spreads halfway open.
Evening clouds heavy with rain hang low across the land.

Rambling tangled in green mountains, all roads surely lost,
I suddenly see a thousand sails come glinting fugitive light.

Following thoughts

Following thoughts all brush-bramble hands open through,
I trace ridgelines, cross creeks, climb out onto terraces beyond:

the simplest wind-and-dew bridge, and this little-boat moon,
lost birds, widowed birds— their comings and goings at an end.

Wang An-shih (1021–1086)

Inscribed on Master Lake-Shadow's Wall

Thatch-eave paths are always well-swept, pure, free of moss,
and with your hands, flowering orchards planted themselves.

A creek meanders by, snug curve cradling jade-green fields.
Two mountains push a door open, and send azure-green inside.

Events at Bushel Mountain

Soundless water, a wandering stream skirts bamboo forest.
And west of bamboo, wildflowers delight in gentle spring.

Facing all this under thatch eaves, I sit through the day.
Not a single bird. No song. Mountain quiet goes deeper still.

Leaving the City

I've lived in the country long enough to know its many joys.
I was starting to feel like a child back in my old village again,

and suddenly, leaving the city today, I leave all that dust behind:
turning to mountains and valleys, I feel them enter my eyes.

Dusk Returns at Bushel Mountain:
Gone to Visit a Master of Way

Through a thousand peaks, ten thousand
peaks beyond, a road travels the flawless.

Blossoms open to bees weaving in and out,
heavy fruit enticing gibbons into trees,

I search for the way across a cold creek.
I was hoping late light would be enough,

but the sky's gone dark, no moon rising.
A houseboy will be out closing the gate.

Sun west and low

Sun west and low: stair-shadow, churning *wu-t'ung* trees.
Blinds raised: green mountains, and half-empty bamboo.

Ducks blurred in fire drift, gold on the chill of deep water.
Dreams a ruins of distance and worry among this birdsong.

In bamboo forest

In bamboo forest, my thatch hut's among stone cliff-roots.
Out front, through thin bamboo, you can glimpse a village.

I doze all day, all idleness. And no one stops by here to visit.
Just this spring wind come sweeping my gate-path clean.

Su Tung-p'o (1037–1101)

Su Tung-p'o (Su Shih) is generally considered the Sung Dynasty's greatest poet, and he may also be its greatest rivers-and-mountains poet. Su was at times quite influential in government, but as he opposed Wang An-shih's radical policies, he spent most of his life in the provinces, including many years in exile. It was this life in the provinces that allowed Su such intimacy with China's rivers and mountains, an intimacy so deep that Su took his literary name, Tung-p'o ("East Slope"), from the site where he lived for some years as a subsistence farmer: East-Slope Su.

But this intimacy was only the starting point for Su's cultivation of wilderness. His poetics dramatically extended the interiorization of wilderness that Mei Yao-ch'en's poetics began. Rather than consciousness giving shape to the world it encounters, Su's poems enact consciousness wandering like water, the operant metaphor for Tao, taking shape according to what it encounters. Su's mastery of this selfless poetics derives in part from his lifelong devotion to Ch'an, for Ch'an no-mind mirrors whatever it encounters with perfect clarity. But as with water, there is an inner nature to the poet which endures through all the transformations. This enduring inner nature returns us to the concept of *li*, or inner pattern, that was so important to Hsieh Ling-yün (see p. 20). And the different roles that *li* plays in these two poets summarize the transformation that had taken place in the rivers-and-mountains tradition.

For Hsieh Ling-yün, *li* was primarily manifested in the empirical world, and the goal of poetry was to render empty mind mirroring the vast dimensions of *li* in the rivers-and-mountains realm. But Su Tung-p'o's poems weave together the empirical world and wandering thought, and for him both aspects are manifestations of *li*, the "inner pattern" of *tzu-jan*'s unfolding. Hence, wilderness is not simply out there in the mountains; it is always already here within us as well. Consciousness is itself already wild—so every gesture in a poem is wilderness, whether it is a turn of thought or a heron taking flight. And in spite of the considerable hardship and political frustration he suffered, this weaving of consciousness into the fabric of wilderness allowed Su a detachment and emotional balance, even lightheartedness, that has endured as part of the Chinese cultural legend.

12th Moon, 14th Sun: A Light Snow Fell Overnight, So I Set Out Early for South Creek, Stopped for a Quick Meal and Arrived Late

Snowfall at South Creek: it's the most priceless of things,
so I set out to see it before it melts. Hurrying my horse,

pushing through thickets alone, I watch for footprints,
and at dawn, I'm first across fresh snow on a red bridge!

Houses in shambles beyond belief, nowhere even to sleep,
I sit facing a village of starvation, voices mere murmurs.

Only the evening crows know my thoughts, startled into
flight, a thousand flakes tumbling through cold branches.

6th Moon, 27th Sun: Sipping Wine at Lake-View Tower

1

Black clouds, soaring ink, nearly blot out these mountains.
White raindrops, skipping pearls, skitter wildly into the boat,

then wind comes across furling earth, scatters them away,
and below Lake-View Tower, lakewater suddenly turns to sky.

2

Setting animals loose —fish and turtles— I'm an exile out here,
but no one owns waterlilies everywhere blooming, blooming.

This lake pillows mountains, starts them glancing up and down,
and my breezy boat wanders free, drifts with an aimless moon.

5

No mere forest recluse, I'm a recluse amid office routines,
mastering idleness that outlasts this idle moment or that.

We have no original home. So where do I go from here?
My old village is nothing like these mountains and lakes.

At Brahma-Heaven Monastery, Following the Rhymes in a Short Poem of Crystalline Beauty by the Monk Acumen-Hoard

You can only hear a bell out beyond mist:
the monastery deep in mist is lost to sight.

Straw sandals wet with the dew of grasses,
a recluse wanders. Never coming to rest,

he's simply an echo of mountaintop moonlight coming and going night after night.

At Seven-Mile Rapids

A light boat one lone leaf,
A startled swan two oars—

water and sky are pure clarity
reflecting deep. Waves smooth,

fish roil this duckweed mirror
and egrets dot misty shorelines.

We breeze past sandy streams,
frostfall streams cold,
moonlit streams aglow,

ridge above ridge like a painting,
bend beyond bend like a screen.

Here I think back to
Yen Tzu-ling's empty old age,

lord and recluse one dream.
Renown's empty then as now,

just mountains stretching away,
cloud mountains erratic,
dawn mountains green.

Su Tung-p'o (1037–1101)

Sipping Wine at the Lake: Skies Start Clearing, Then Rain

It's gorgeous under clearing skies, a lake all billows and light,
and lovely too in rain, mountain colors among empty mists.

I can't help comparing West Lake to Lady West, her makeup
just barely there or laid on thick: she's exquisite either way.

Visiting Beckons-Away Monastery

Walking, I sing of ridgelines in white cloud,
and sitting, chant hymns to bamboo orchards.

Blossoms falling even without much breeze,
mountains half shadow under a fading sun:

who could make out the creek's wildflowers
in all this dark, or trace their fragrant scents?

Whenever I see people who ply city markets,
I realize recluse sorrows don't go very deep.

There's a Small Monastery on the Cragged Heights of Blue-Ox Ridge, a Place Human Tracks Rarely Reach

Hurrying our horses home last night, passing river dikes of sand,
we found kitchen smoke trailing fragrance out across ten miles,

and this morning we wander Blue-Ox Ridge, walking sticks in hand,
cliffwall cascades drumming the silence of a thousand mountains.

Don't laugh at the old monk.
It's true he's deaf as dragons,
but at the end of this hundred-year life, who isn't a pitiful sight?

And tomorrow morning, long after we've set out again for the city,
he'll still be here among the white clouds of this poem on the wall.

With Mao and Fang, Visiting Bright-Insight Monastery

It's enough on this twisting mountain road to simply stop.
Clear water cascades thin down rock, startling admiration,

white cloud swells of itself across ridgelines east and west,
and who knows if the lake's bright moon is above or below?

It's the season black and yellow millet both begin to ripen,
oranges red and green, halfway into such lovely sweetness.

All this joy in our lives— what is it but heaven's great gift?
Why confuse the children with all our fine explanations?

Su Tung-p'o (1037—1101)

After Li Szu-hsün's Painting, Cragged Islands
on the Yangtze

Mountains all azure green,
the river all boundless away,
Lone-Spires loom up out of the water, Greater beside Lesser,

and the road ends among fallen cliffwalls, gibbons and birds
scattered away, then nothing but trees towering up into sky.

Where's that river-trader sailing from?
Its oar-songs rise and fall midstream in the river's current

as a gentle breeze plays across shoreline sand, too faint to see.
And Lone-Spires always plunge and swell with passing boats:

majestic summits two slave-girls in mist,
they adorn themselves in dawn's mirror.

That merchant there on the boat— he's hardly mean and cruel.
Year before last, his housegirl married an awfully handsome man.

Midsummer Festival, Wandering Up
as Far as the Monastery

I was going wherever I happened to go,
giving myself over to whatever I met,

when incense drew my recluse steps to
mats spread open and pure, tea poured.

Light rain delayed my return, quiet
mystery outside windows lovelier still:

bowl-dome summits blocking out sun,
grasses and trees turned shadowy green.

Climbing quickly to the highest shrine,
I gazed out across whole Buddha-realms,

city walls radiant beneath Helmet Peak
and cloudy skies adrift in Tremor Lake.

Such joy in all this depth and clarity,
such freedom in wide-open mountains,

my recluse search wasn't over when dusk
cook-smoke rose above distant villages.

Back home now, this day held in mind
shines bright and clear. I can't sleep,

and those monks are sitting awake too,
sharing a lamp's light in *ch'an* stillness.

**With the Wang Brothers and My Son Mai,
I Wander City Walls, Gazing at Waterlily
Blossoms, Then Climb to the Pavilion on
Grand-View Mountain, Finally Returning
at Dusk to Petals-Flight Monastery**

This clear wind— what kind of thing is it?
Something you can love but never name,

it goes wherever it goes, like a noble sage,
fills grasses and trees with lovely sounds.

We set out wandering without any purpose,
and then, letting our lone boat drift askew,

we're midstream on our backs, gazing into
sky and exchanging greetings with wind.

Offering a toast to water spread boundless
away, I savor this indifference we share,

and all the way home, along both rivers,
clouds and water shimmer into the night.

At Red Cliffs, Thinking of Ancient Times

The great river flows east,
its current rinsing
all those gallant figures of a thousand ages away.

West of the ancient battlements,
people say, are
the Red Cliffs of young Chou from the Three Kingdoms:

a confusion of rock piercing sky
and wild waves pounding cliffwalls,
roiling up into a thousand swells of snow.

It's like a painting, river and mountains
where how many august heroes once came together,
and I can almost see it back then, when Lord Chou was
here with lovely Ch'iao, his young new bride:

his bright and fearless presence
with feather fan and silk turban,
talking and laughing
as masts and hulls became flying ash and vanished smoke.

Surely spirits of that ancient time
roam here, smiling at all these feelings
and my hair already turning white.
Our life's like dream,
so pour out the whole cup, offering to a river and its moon.

Su Tung-p'o (1037–1101)

Partridge Sky

Forests end in mountain light, and bamboo hides walls.
A confusion of cicada cries, dry grasses, a small pond.

An occasional bird wings white through empty sky,
and delicate in scent, waterlilies shine across water.

Out beyond the village, along
ancient city walls, I'll stroll
till dusk, staff in hand, then turn back in slant light.

Thanks to rain that came last night in the third watch,
I get another cool day in this drifting dream of a life.

Presented to Abbot Perpetua All-Gathering at East-Forest Monastery

A murmuring stream is the tongue broad and unending,
and what is mountain color if not the body pure and clear?

Eighty-four thousand *gathas* fill a passing night. But still,
once day has come, how could I explain them to anyone?

Inscribed on a Wall at Thatch-Hut Mountain's East-Forest Monastery

Seen from one side, it's a ridgeline. From another, it's a peak.
Distant or near, high or low— it never looks the same twice.

If I don't recognize the contours of Thatch-Hut's true face,
here's why: I'm right here in the midst of these mountains!

Inscribed on a Painting in Wang Ting-kuo's Collection
Entitled Misty River and Crowded Peaks

Heartbreak above the river, a thousand peaks and summits
drift kingfisher-green in empty skies, like mist and cloud.

At these distances, you don't know if it's mountain or cloud
until mist thins away and clouds scatter. Then mountains

remain, filling sight with canyoned cliffwalls, azure-
green, valleys in cragged shadow,
and cascades tumbling a hundred Ways in headlong flight,

stitching forests and threading rock, seen and then unseen
as they plunge toward valley headwaters, and wild streams

growing calm where mountains open out and forests end.
A small bridge and country inn nestled against mountains,

travelers gradually work their way beyond towering trees,
and a fishing boat drifts, lone leaf on a river swallowing sky.

I can't help asking where you found a painting like this,
bottomless beauty and clarity so lavish in exquisite detail:

I never dreamed there was a place in this human
realm so perfect, so lovely.
All I want is to go there, buy myself a few acres and settle in.

You can almost see them, can't you? Those pure and remote
places in Wu-ch'ang and Fan-k'ou
where I lingered out five recluse years as Master East-Slope:

a river trembling in spring wind, isolate skies boundless,
and evening clouds furling rain back across lovely peaks,

crows gliding out of red maples to share a boatman's night
and snow tumbling off tall pines startling his midday sleep.

Su Tung-p'o (1037–1101)

Peach blossoms drift streamwater away right here in this
human realm, and Savage-Knoll wasn't for spirit immortals.

Rivers and mountains all empty clarity: there's a road in,
but caught in the dust of this world, I'll never find it again.

Returning your painting, I'm taken by sighs of sad wonder.
I have old friends in those mountains,
                              and their poems keep calling me home.

Crossing the Mountains

Seven years wandering hither and yon: it's too much to bear,
but here I ladle a first sweet taste of Hui Neng's streamwater.

In dream it seems that I once went to live out beyond the sea,
but after a little wine, I've never come south of the Yangtze.

Water rinses my feet, an empty mountain stream murmuring,
and mist drifts into my robes, all droplets of kingfisher-green.

Who can let go of a mountain pheasant breaking into flight
across cliffwalls, blossom and rain and feathers trailing down?

Su Tung-p'o (1037–1101)

Lu Yu (1125–1210)

The Sung interiorization of wilderness came to another of its logical conclusions in the late work of Lu Yu. After a tempestuous and undistinguished government career, a time during which close bonds of friendship formed between Lu Yu and the other two major poets of the late Sung, Fan Ch'eng-ta and Yang Wan-li, Lu Yu retired to spend his last two decades as an increasingly impoverished recluse on a farm at his ancestral village in Shao-hsing. There, his long practice of Ch'an no-mind coming to fruition, he cultivated a profound transparency to experience: during these two decades he wrote no less than 6,500 poems (about one per day), which he arranged chronologically in his collection. This engagement had already led Lu Yu to write a celebrated mountain-travel diary that was unprecedented for its size and exhaustive detail, and it gives his poetic oeuvre the feel of a notebook or journal tracing the wanderings of a person's attention through the days and seasons of a life.

It is remarkable how consistently successful Lu Yu's poems are in the traditional sense of rendering a compelling poetic statement. But the mastery of the poems lies more in their form than in any particular statement they make, for they are quintessential Sung: rather than *portray* insight, they *enact* it. Lu Yu was beyond the need to distill or intensify experience into a privileged moment of insight. Instead, Lu's poems have a texture of idle contentment deriving from his understanding that ordinary experience is always already enlightened, and wilderness resides as much in the everyday movement of perception and reflection as in high peaks and valleys. So transparency as the day-to-day form of life represents Lu Yu's distinctive way of weaving consciousness into the fabric of wilderness, making every gesture in a poem wild.

To suggest this day-to-day form of transparency, the poems translated here are a consecutive sequence from an arbitrarily chosen moment in Lu Yu's life: a few days in the autumn of 1205, Lu Yu's 80th year.

The River Village

What a joke that scholar's office cap was. Not another word:
my hair's white now, and I'm happy dozing in a river village,

though birds roosting in deep forests call one after another,
and boats moving through locks kick up that racket all night.

I'm sick, but get up and rummage all day in tattered old books,
and when sorrow comes, I just pour a little crystalline wine,

but how secluded is this life anyway? Just listen to this place!
It's late, and still some monk's out knocking at a moonlit gate!

Lu Yu (1125–1210)

A Mountain Walk

Heading south from my brushwood gate, I start climbing
this mountain, grass sandals tattered among white clouds,

forgetting I'm so poor I may never repay my wine debts.
Ignoring a monk's stone inscription, I abide in idleness,

my ancient three-foot *ch'in* a last trace of cook-smoke,
my *ch'an* staff a lone tree-limb of Hsiang River ripples.

I gaze north from my little hut here, into mist and cloud,
friends all scattered away, birds returning for the night.

Following the Trail Up from Deva-King Monastery to the Guesthouse Where My Friend Wang Chung-hsin and I Wrote Our Names on a Wall Fifty Years Ago, I Find the Names Still There

Meandering these greens, azure all around, you plumb antiquity.
East of the wall, above the river, stands this ancient monastery,

its thatched halls we visited so long ago: you a mountain sage
and I here from Wei River northlands, half drunk and writing.

Painted paddle still, I drift awhile free. Then soon, I'm nearing
home, azure walking-stick in hand, my recluse search ending.

Old friends dead and gone, their houses in ruins, I walk through
thick bamboo, deep cloud, each step a further step into confusion.

Off-Hand Poem at My East Window

I pass the whole day in utter tranquillity at my east window,
all that mirage and illusion of a lifetime gone, mind empty.

Autumn *ch'i* isn't baring trees yet. But I'm old, and already
thinking of that first time I felt the hundred insects calling.

The ridges of a folding screen recall Thatch-Hut mountains,
and my wife's high-peaked hat sacred Little-Forest summits,

but how could that flush of young health and strength last?
A vine follows the contours, recluse quiet wherever it goes.

7th Moon, 29th Sun, Yi Year of the Ox: I Had a Dream
Last Night in Which I Met a Stately Man, and at First
Sight We Were Like Old Friends. He Had Written Pages
of Lovely Poems Long Ago, All Perfectly Pure and Simple.
I Started Reading Through Them, but Woke Before I
Could Finish. To Record What Happened, I've Written
This in Long Lines.

The traveler is an instant friend, utterly clear and true:
even before we dip out wine, we share kindred thoughts.

The pillow is cold, but I don't understand it's all a dream
in the clear night. I just savor that vision of an old sage.

Star River tipped, Dipper sunk, ancient histories empty,
mist scatters and clouds leave. Our two bodies are mirage,

and mind is perfect clarity. It sees through this illusion.
Awake, you can't avoid it: all things the same bittersweet.

To My Son, Yü

An old-timer's just a worn-out child. I can't manage alone.
Though this mind is companion to sage ancient masters,

everything's gone: firewood, water, servants, strength.
And I've even pawned my *ch'in* and books. It's that bad.

Mortar and pestle are silent: I'm too sick to grind medicine.
The granary's swept out: there's nervous talk of hunger.

I still have a few years left. You'll need to look after me.
Those misty ten-thousand-mile views will just have to wait.

Light Rain

Blazing summer days: no force could bring them back.
Clouds suddenly rising off the river, lovely, so lovely,

ducks leave a bridge's shadow, paddling into fine rain,
and butterflies flutter out, frolicking in field breezes.

The willow won't survive nights and days much longer,
and waterlilies will only open two or three more times.

If the changing sights of a single year haunt your eye,
why wonder that a palace lake is ash among the kalpas?

On a Boat

1

A three-plank boat, its sail made of ragged bamboo mats,
a fishing lantern anchored overnight at heaven's gate:

forty-eight thousand acres of misty lakewater, where
the Maker-of-Things hurries narcissus flocks into bloom.

2

Scents of mountain vegetables and tender herbs everywhere,
the view's regal down to sheep coddled for the emperor's table.

I trust my thoughts to that voice of the ancient Liu Wen-shu:
it's soy gruel that's always been the most enduring of flavors.

Fan Ch'eng-ta (1126–1193)

Fan Ch'eng-ta lived until his twenty-eighth year as a relatively poor recluse, studying poetry and practicing Ch'an at his family farm on the shores of Stone Lake in southeast China. He only reluctantly entered government service, but in spite of his ongoing reluctance, he had a successful career involving considerable travel among the rivers and mountains of China. Nevertheless, he eventually retired back to his ancestral farm in the tamer landscapes of Stone Lake, and the focus of his poetry likewise moved from rivers and mountains to the more domestic perspective of village fields and gardens for which his poetry is best known. At Stone Lake, Fan cultivated an intimacy with natural process that verges on identification, an intimacy apparent not only in his poems, but also in his choice of "Stone Lake" for a literary name: Stone-Lake Fan.

Fan's most famous work in this domestic mode is his "Four Seasons Among Fields and Gardens," a sequence of sixty short poems tracing the life of his mountain village through the seasons. In structuring his sequence of poems according to the seasonal cycle, Fan emphasizes deep wilderness as the context of daily life, for the wilderness cosmology of being and non-being is nowhere so clearly manifest as in the seasonal cycle: winter's empty nonbeing, spring's burgeoning forth, summer's fullness, and autumn's return to pregnant emptiness. And as the poem attends equally to both the human and nonhuman, it weaves them together in the fabric of that wilderness cosmology.

The sequence also enacts this integration at the immediate level of consciousness. Typical of Fan's later Stone Lake poems, it is infused with the clarity of Ch'an no-mind. Unlike Su Tung-p'o and Lu Yu, whose poems weave the empirical world together with the movements of thought, the "Four Seasons" sequence presents a picture of events in his farming village that is rich with realistic detail and rarely clouded by his own thoughts or feelings. This is a fully achieved realization of the sagely Ch'an clarity that has been central to rivers-and-mountains poetry since Wang Wei. It is especially compelling here, for it focuses on the quotidian where we actually live our daily lives, rather than stretching for grand landscapes and profound insights. And often containing a surprising turn or clarity of image that suggests a kind of Ch'an awakening, the poems generously open us to the no-mind transparency that suffuses them and is our deepest form of belonging to the Cosmos.

Midstream at Thorn-Bramble Island, I Turn to Look Back at Shaman Mountain and Find Nothing There

Inside Triple Gorge, beneath a thousand, ten thousand peaks,
you can't believe there's level ground anywhere people know,

but seen from Island Palace ruins, it's all water merged into sky,
and you're sure the world's been flat and mountainless forever.

Rivers and mountains that once greeted me now bid farewell:
a turn of the head and they've simply vanished. It's like a dream:

of ten thousand miles back home, three thousand flew by today,
the dream turning to journey's end on the shores of Stone Lake.

Four Seasons Among Fields and Gardens

Spring

Willow blossoms deep in the lane, a rooster calls out at noon.
Young mulberry leaves are still sharp and less than green.

I sit dozing, then wake. Nothing at all to do, I watch where
blue-sky sunlight fills the window: silkworms hatching out.

Wheat and barley in high fields blend into mountain blues,
and along the river, low fields are still green and unplowed.

Peach and apricot fill the village, a spring brocade in bloom,
and Bright-Clarity Festival: feet dance to song, drums throb.

Late Spring

Thirty days of quiet for the silkworms: our gates stay closed
and the village paths empty. Not a human track anywhere

until this morning of clear skies, wind, dew. Today the day
we gather mulberry leaves, neighbors spot neighbors again.

Crows make their way back toward forests. Visitors here rare,
misty shadow spreads from mountains to our brushwood gate.

A lone boy with a single paddle, his boat out there like a leaf:
he weaves himself into evening dark, ducks filing back home.

Summer

You have to dump water out of low fields into the river,
or force it up impossible channels onto the high ridges.

The land's far from level here, wears people to the bone.
It goes on and on: men trudging atop water-lift wheels.

Harvesting water chestnuts is bitter. Plow and hoe useless,
starveling bodies ghostly, fingers bleed streams of red.

No money to buy fieldland, all they can do is farm water.
And now there's someone charging rent on lakewater too!

Autumn

Wolfberry and chrysanthemum dangle pearls, drip dew red.
Two crickets sing back and forth, chatting in sedge thickets.

Silkworm threads are tangled across yellow sunflower leaves,
silence deserted, the towering blossoms tipped in dusk wind.

Freshly pounded clay, the threshing-yard smooth as a mirror.
Our families all pound at rice while frost-clear weather holds,

then tonight, amid the song and laughter, faint thunder stirs.
Flails hardly pause all night: that throbbing through til dawn.

Winter

A slant-light sun sinks into mountains. A sliver of moon drifts.
Sleep lingering, I wander river country to ease medicine in,

frost-edged winds tearing a thousand forests of leaves away.
Propped on my bamboo staff, all idleness, I count crane nests.

Idle, my boat adrift, I gaze into mountain peaks all sunlit snow.
Winds settle. Their chill lingers. Then at nightfall, it turns icy.

I sit listening to the oar shatter through pearl and splinter jade.
I didn't know. This lakewater— it's already spawned a skin of ice!

Yang Wan-li (1127–1206)

Yang Wan-li represents a culmination of Ch'an poetics in rivers-and-mountains poetry. Although he had a successful official career—a trusted advisor to prime ministers and emperors at times, and at others banished to the provinces—Yang was always a very serious Ch'an practitioner, and he had a more thoroughly Ch'an conception of poetry than any other poet in the tradition. Like a Ch'an adept practicing directly under Ch'an masters, Yang studied assiduously with the poetic masters of the past, trying to match his poetic insights to theirs; until finally, at the age of fifty, this "practice" led to a moment of sudden enlightenment. Throwing over his ties to the literary tradition, he began working spontaneously in his own style from immediate experience, and *tzu-jan* seemed to present itself to him in poems that virtually wrote themselves. His poems were thereafter written with a kind of selfless spontaneity, a procedure which itself wove him into natural process.

Yang's poetic enlightenment seems to have been part of a broader Ch'an enlightenment, and this awakening is reflected in the poems themselves. A typical Yang poem in the rivers-and-mountains mode attends to the passing moments of immediate experience with a resounding clarity, and this attention usually leads to a moment of sudden enlightenment: a startling image or turn of thought, a surprising imaginative gesture, a sudden twist of humor. But the depths of Yang's enlightenment were such that he could make poems out of nothing more than that crystalline attention to things themselves. The rivers-and-mountains realm was the natural terrain for this attentiveness, as its grandeur so easily calls one from the limitations of self to the expansiveness of a mirror-like empty mind that contains all things. But more often than any other poet, Yang also attends to the most mundane aspects of wilderness—empty mind completely occupied with nothing special: a fly, for instance, sunning on a windowsill.

* * *

Yang Wan-li was the last of the great Sung poets, and with him China's rivers-and-mountains poetry had opened up virtually all of its possibilities. China's poets would continue to actively cultivate this rich terrain up to the present, but there would be few truly fundamental innovations. This is perhaps a testament to the profundity of this tradition, for once the terms of our dwelling within this wilderness cosmology are established, we can simply settle into our mountain home, our poetry becoming a way of steadily deepening the gift of that dwelling.

With Chün Yü and Chi Yung, I Hike to Universal-Completion Monastery—Then Return Late, Sailing Across West Lake

1

The screen's shade is faint, too faint to hide clear skies,
and a goosefoot staff is keeping me fresh. It's time to go,

but lakeside mountains have gracious plans to keep me,
leaving distant bells silent, sound itself as yet unknown.

2

As our boat lacing mists angles off the cove's willow shores,
cloud mountains appear and disappear among the willows.

And the beauty of climbing a mountain while adrift on a lake?
It's this lake's mind— that gaze holding the mountain utterly.

A Cold Fly

Chance sight on a windowsill, the fly sits warming its back,
rubbing its front legs together, savoring morning sunlight.

Sun nudges shadow closer. But the fly knows what's coming,
and suddenly it's gone— a *buzz* heading for the next window.

Cold Sparrows

A hundred thousand sparrows descend on my empty courtyard.
A few gather atop the plums, chatting with clear evening skies,

and the rest swarm around, trying to murder me with their racket.
Suddenly they all startle away, and there's silence: not a sound.

Yang Wan-li (1127–1206)

Breakfast at Noonday-Ascension Mountain

These thousand peaks offer the beauties of spring again,
and what do I offer them? Nothing but mounting alarm.

Clouds plunder cragged cliffs where birds sing in trees,
rain swells mountain streams, cascades scattering petals,

and I can't see past thatch roofs, a wisp of kitchen smoke,
but I know exactly how starvation will look in this village.

I knew there'd be no meat for breakfast. But they barely
even manage bamboo shoots: just two or three grams each.

On a Boat Crossing Hsieh Lake

I pour out a cup or two of emerald wine inside the cabin.
The door swings closed, then back open onto exquisite

ranged mountains: ten thousand wrinkles unseen by anyone,
and every ridge hand-picked by the late sun's slant light.

Night Rain at Luster Gap

The gorge's river all empty clarity, rain sweeps in,
cold breezy whispers beginning deep in the night,

and ten thousand pearls start clattering on a plate,
each one's *tic* a perfect clarity piercing my bones.

I scratch my head in dream, then get up and listen
till dawn, hearing each sound appear and disappear.

I've listened to rain all my life. My hair's white now,
and I still don't know night rain on a spring river.

Overnight at East Island

2

To see them, look at mountains revealed and unrevealed.
If you don't, even looking at mountains is pure delusion.

Ten thousand peaks of blue keep me enthralled all day,
and at dusk, I linger out twilight's last few purple spires,

but of those sightseers coming and going on riverboats,
gazing out at mountains, how many see them absolutely?

Let those boatmen keep their reckless talk to themselves:
if you scare the children, they'll refuse to go anywhere.

3

Always wanting to fill a poet's eyes to the brim, old heaven
worries that autumn mountains are too washed-out and dead,

so it measures out Shu brocade, unfurls flushed clouds of Wu,
and rubs them lush and low across these autumn mountains.

Before long, red brocade thins into kingfisher-green gauze
as heaven's loom weaves out evening crows returning home,

then evening crows and kingfisher-green gauze are gone:
nothing in sight but a clear river pure as sun-bleached silk.

Crossing Open-Anew Lake

A fisherman's taking his boat deep across the lake.
My old eyes trace his path all the way, his precise

wavering in and out of view. Then it gets strange:
suddenly he's a lone goose balanced on a bent reed.

At Hsieh Cove

The ox path I'm on ends in a rabbit trail, and suddenly
I'm facing open plains and empty sky on all four sides.

My thoughts follow white egrets— a pair taking flight,
leading sight across a million blue mountains rising

ridge beyond ridge, my gaze lingering near then far,
enthralled by peaks crowded together or there alone.

Even a hill or valley means thoughts beyond knowing—
and all this? A crusty old man's now a wide-eyed child!

The Small Pond

A spring's eye of shadow resists even the slightest flow.
Among tree shadow, its lit water adores warm clear skies.

Spiral of blades, a tiny waterlily's clenched against dew,
and there at the very tip, in early light, sits a dragonfly.

Yang Wan-li (1127–1206)

On the Summit Above Tranquil-Joy Temple

Who says poets are so enthralled with mountains? Mountains,
mountains, mountains— I've raved on and on, and they're still

clamoring for attention. A thousand peaks, ten thousand ridges:
it's too much for me. If I climb an hour, I need to rest for three.

When your desk is piled full, you just can't add anything more,
and when your withered stomach is full, who can keep eating?

So what good's even a faint scrap of mist or kingfisher-green?
I'll wrap it all up, send the whole bundle off to my city friends.

Notes

T'ao Ch'ien

6   *Thatch-Hut Mountain:* Beginning with T'ao Ch'ien's residence on its northwest slopes, Thatch-Hut (Hermitage) Mountain (Lu Mountain) was a major
site in the rivers-and-mountains tradition, recurring often in the work of T'ao's
descendants.

8   *wine:* In Chinese poetry, the practice of wine generally means drinking just
enough wine to achieve a serene clarity of attention, a state in which the isola-
tion of a mind imposing distinctions on the world gives way to a sense of identity with the world. Indeed, poets such as Po Chü-i half-seriously spoke of wine
rivaling Ch'an as a spiritual practice. See also Introduction, p. xvi.

9   *gates:* Throughout the recluse tradition, "gate" often carries the metaphoric
sense of "awareness," that through which the empirical world enters consciousness. Hence, "within these gates" is not only T'ao Ch'ien's solitary house (the
gate would have been in the wall or fence that surrounded the courtyard of his
house), but his mind as well. This added dimension harks back to a passage in
Chapter 52 of the *Tao Te Ching* that is describing a kind of meditative practice:

> If you block the senses
> and close the gate,
> you never struggle.
> If you open the senses
> and expand your endeavors,
> nothing can save you.

The idea of "closing the gate" became a familiar motif in recluse poetry (see
pp. 72, 218), the literal point being that their house was very secluded and they
were content in that seclusion, rather than longing for company. Other equally
resonant motifs include: leaving the gate open (pp. 34, 107) and sweeping the
gate-path as a gesture of welcome for unexpected guests (pp. 63, 220). And see
Key Terms, *hsien*, for the role "gate" plays in the pictograph rendering that
central spiritual posture, idleness.

dust: Insubstantial worldly affairs.

empty: See Key Terms: *k'ung.*

idleness: See Key Terms: *hsien.*

occurrence coming of itself: See Key Terms: *tzu-jan.*

13   *mind:* See Key Terms: *hsin.*

chrysanthemum: Closely associated with T'ao Ch'ien in the Chinese imagination, chrysanthemums were popularly imagined to promote longevity because
they bloom in autumn and their blossoms are especially long-lasting.

South Mountain: Calling up such passages as "like the timelessness of South
Mountain" in *The Book of Songs* (*Shih Ching*, 166/6), South Mountain came to
have a kind of mythic stature as the embodiment of the elemental and timeless

nature of the earth. Given this pedigree, poets often used this name to refer to whatever mountain happened to be south of them. In this case, it is Thatch-Hut Mountain. See p. 19 for T'ao Ch'ien's other famous use of this term.

16   *9/9:* The 9ᵗʰ day of the 9ᵗʰ lunar month, a holiday dominated by thoughts of mortality held on this day because the word for "9" *(chiu)* is pronounced the same as the word meaning "long-lasting," hence *"ever and ever."* The holiday was celebrated by climbing to a mountaintop and drinking chrysanthemum wine.

17   **Cha** *Festival:* Ancient name for the *La* Festival, which in T'ao's time fell on the last day of the lunar year. It was the first day of New Year festivities celebrating the arrival of spring. In ancient China, New Year's Day was not only the earth's "birth day," as it was the first day of spring, but the birthday of all the people in China, each of whom added a year to their age on this day.

18   *5ᵗʰ* **Moon:** The Chinese calendar follows the lunar cycles, and the word for "month" is "moon" *(yüeh)*.
     inner pattern: See Key Terms: *li*.
     Hua or Sung: Two of China's five sacred mountains, often climbed by pilgrims.

19   In China, graves were placed on hillsides.

Hsieh Ling-yün

24   *Ch'i-Sited:* It was thought that different features of a landscape determine the movement of *ch'i*, the universal breath. The best site for a house would be determined by a diviner who analyzed how the local movements of *ch'i* harmonized with the particular characteristics of those who were to live in the house.
     adoration: See p. 20.

25   *heaven:* See Key Terms: *t'ien*.
     Ch'ü Yüan: China's first major poet, Ch'ü Yüan (340–278 B.C.E.) wrote a number of the poems in the *Ch'u Tz'u (Songs of the South)* anthology. He was unjustly exiled, and in his grief threw himself into a river and drowned.
     Yüeh Yi: Like Hsieh's grandfather (Hsieh Hsüan) and Ch'ü Yüan, Yüeh Yi was a national hero who fell out of favor with his sovereign. Once the sovereign had turned against him because of slanders, Yüeh Yi decided to leave the country rather than risk execution.

26   *Master Pan:* Pan Szu (c. 1ˢᵗ c. B.C.E.–1ˢᵗ c. C.E.), a Taoist recluse known for his profound sayings.
     Master Shang: A recluse who was finally coaxed into taking government office because of his extreme poverty. He served reluctantly and finally left to end his life traveling among China's famous mountains.

37   *Thatch-Hut Mountain:* Thatch-Hut Mountain (see note to p. 6) was also a major monastic center. Among the many monasteries on Thatch-Hut Mountain, East-Forest was the most famous. It was founded there by Hui Yüan (334–416 C.E.), a major figure in Chinese Buddhism who emphasized *dhyāna* (sitting meditation), as he taught a form of Buddhism that contained early

glimmers of Ch'an (*ch'an* is the Chinese translation of *dhyāna*). Hui Yüan was a contemporary of T'ao Ch'ien and Hsieh Ling-yün. T'ao Ch'ien lived nearby and visited Hui Yüan numerous times; and according to legend it was a visit to East-Forest that first aroused Hsieh's devotion to Buddhist practice.

Ellipses indicate lacunae in the text.

dragon: As benevolent as it is destructive, the Chinese dragon is both feared and revered as the awesome force of life itself. Animating all things and in constant transformation, it descends into deep waters in autumn, where it hibernates until spring, when it rises. Because the dragon embodies the spirit of change, its awakening is equivalent to the awakening of spring and the return of life to earth.

Meng Hao-jan

45   *Mei Fu . . . Po Lüan:* Legendary recluses from the 1st century C.E.

     Wu and Kuei: The ancient lands of Wu and Kuei had been unified as Wu-Kuei.

46   *dark-enigma:* See Key Terms: *hsüan.*

47   *Incense-Burner Peak . . . Hui Yüan . . . East-Forest:* Incense-Burner is one of the two major peaks in the Thatch-Hut Mountain complex just south of Hsün-yang (see note to p. 6). For Hui Yüan and East-Forest Monastery, see note to p. 37.

48   *ch'an:* Ch'an is the Chinese translation of *dhyāna,* Sanskrit for "sitting meditation." The Ch'an Buddhist sect takes that name because it focuses so resolutely on sitting meditation.

50   *Master P'ang:* A fabled recluse from the 2nd century C.E., Master P'ang lived on Deer-Gate Mountain and never entered cities or took office.

     white cloud: This image of white clouds recurs often in the rivers-and-mountains tradition. It simultaneously describes an empty and free state of mind, the sense of secluded distances, and the sense of drifting free like a cloud.

53   *Jung:* Abbot of Lumen-Empty Monastery just south of Hsiang-yang, on White-Horse Mountain, Jung was a long-time friend and Ch'an teacher of Meng Hao-jan.

Wang Wei

59   *P'ei Ti:* P'ei Ti was Wang Wei's closest friend and kindred spirit. This friendship is famous for the poetic exchanges that resulted when they were together in the mountains. One would write a poem, then the other would try to write one that echoes or responds in some way to the first. "Wheel-Rim River Sequence" is a particularly well-known example, as is this set where Wang Wei is responding to the following poem that P'ei Ti had just written:

> **Caught in Rain at Wheel-Rim River's Source,**
> **Thinking of Whole-South Mountain**
>
> Clouds darken the river's meandering
> emptiness. Colors adrift end in sand.

Wheel-Rim River flows distant away,
and where is Whole-South Mountain?

60 **Wheel-Rim River Sequence:** Wang Wei spent periods of seclusion throughout his life in many different places—but in his middle years he acquired his famous Wheel-Rim River (Wang River) retreat in the Whole-South mountains, just south of the capital, Ch'ang-an. It was there that the conjunction of Wang's painting and poetry coalesced in his famous Wheel-Rim River Sequence and a corresponding scroll painting: probably his best-known poem and painting.

rebuilt house: Sung Chih-wen, a well-known poet, had owned the house before Wang Wei. Sung had died about thirty years before Wang bought the house, and the house had been left unused in the interim.

66 **ch'in:** The ancient stringed instrument that Chinese poets used to accompany the chanting of their poems (poems were always sung), the *ch'in* appears often in classical poetry. It is ancestor to the more familiar Japanese *koto*.

settle into breath chants: A method of harmonizing oneself with natural process.

67 *sangha:* A community of Buddhist practitioners.

72 *close my bramble gate:* See note to p. 9.

Li Po

76 **Star River:** The Milky Way.

Change-Maker: Tao.

84 **East-Forest Monastery:** See note to p. 37.

kalpas: A kalpa is a cosmic cycle extending from the creation of a world-system to its destruction—traditionally given as 4,320,000 years.

91 *Hsieh T'iao:* Major 5th c. poet remembered for his rivers-and-mountains poems.

Tu Fu

96 **The nation falls into ruins . . . :** This line has recently been rewritten to reflect our contemporary reality: "Rivers and mountains fall into ruins; the state continues."

97 **Sacred Peak:** There is one sacred mountain for each direction in China, and one at the center. Exalt (Tai) Mountain in the east is the most sacred of these five sacred mountains.

101 *watch:* There were five watches in a night, two hours each, beginning at 7 p.m. and ending at 5 a.m.

103 *ch'i:* The universal breath, vital energy, or life-giving principle.

fulling-stone: Fulling (thickening) heavy cloth to make winter clothes for conscripted soldiers fighting far away was a kind of grief-filled autumn ritual for the women who were left alone at home.

104 **Triple Gorge:** A set of three spectacular gorges formed where the Yangtze River cut its way through the formidable Shaman (Wu) Mountains, forming a two-hundred-mile stretch of very narrow canyons. Famous for the river's violence

and the towering cliffs haunted by shrieking gibbons, the gorges appear often in Chinese poetry. They were located on the very outskirts of the civilized world, in a part of south China inhabited primarily by aboriginal peoples, and frequently encountered by traveling (often exiled) artist-intellectuals. Tu Fu was living at K'uei-chou, which overlooked the first of the three gorges. As this book goes to press, a huge hydroelectric project at Triple Gorge is nearing completion: when finished, the dam will completely inundate these magnificent gorges.

Slumber-Dragon, Leap-Stallion: Chu-ko Liang and Pai-ti, well-known figures from Chinese history—the first of whom was a great cultural hero and the latter an infamous villain.

106 **Musk Deer:** Very small animals, averaging only two feet in height, and very timid. In our time, musk deer have been slaughtered in the wild by the hundreds of thousands not for food, but for their musk oil (each male having only one teaspoon of oil), which is used in fine perfumes.

110 **Lo-yang:** One of the two capitals in the north, Lo-yang was by now devastated, having been overrun twice by rebel armies and recaptured twice by loyal armies. Tu Fu's friend, Meng, had left Lo-yang to search for his old village, which was almost certainly destroyed by the fighting.

Wei Ying-wu

121 **Twin-Stream:** Located in the deep south, this is the monastery of Hui-neng (638–713), the Sixth Patriarch—author of the Platform Sutra and revered as one of the two great figures in the founding of Ch'an.

124 **white-stone soup:** Legendary fare for the pure and impoverished recluse, named after a fabled recluse Master White-Stones.

Cold Mountain (Han Shan)

129 **Way:** Tao, meaning both "path or road" and Lao Tzu's Tao. See Key Terms: Tao.

135 **wandering boundless and free:** This phrase recurs in Chuang Tzu. It is the title of Chapter 1, and section 11 of Chapter 6 includes this description of two sages:

> On loan from everything else, they'll soon be entrusted back to the one body. Forgetting liver and gallbladder, abandoning ears and eyes, they'll continue on again, tumbling and twirling through a blur of endings and beginnings. They roam at ease beyond the tawdry dust of this world, nothing's own doing [wu-wei] wandering boundless and free through the selfless unfolding of things.

137 **no-mind:** Mind emptied of self and its constructions of the world. In this state, a goal of Ch'an practice, nonbeing as empty mind mirrors the ten thousand things. See also p. 57.

Meng Chiao

143 *Triple Gorge:* see note to p. 104.

144 *dragons:* See note to p. 37.

146 *Death-owls call:* The Chinese thought an owl's voice resembled that of a ghost or spirit, so they thought a calling owl was calling the spirit of a dying person away.

Liu Tsung-yüan

152 *28ᵗʰ sun . . . 9ᵗʰ moon:* Just as the word for "month" is "moon" in Chinese, the word for "day" is "sun."

Maker-of-Things: Tao or *tzu-jan.*

153 The close of this essay echoes ideas that suffuse the *Chuang Tzu,* as in passages such as that in the note to p. 135, or these from Chapter 1, sections 10 and 12:

> But if you mount the source of heaven and earth and the ten thousand changes, if you ride the six seasons of *ch'i* in their endless dispute, then you travel the inexhaustible, depending on nothing at all.

> A man of such Integrity ranges far and wide through the ten thousand things, mingling with them into one vast embrace of change.

Po Chü-i

166 There is also a celebrated prose version of this poem: "Record of a Thatched Hut." It is available in Burton Watson's *Four Huts* and Richard Strassberg's *Inscribed Landscapes.*

174 *Duke Liu:* After being instrumental in the founding of the Han Dynasty, Duke Liu (Chang Liang: c. 200 B.C.E.) became an assiduous recluse.

Master Red Pine: After magically summoning heavy rains and saving the empire from drought, the legendary Red Pine (c. 27ᵗʰ century B.C.E.) was transformed into an immortal and lived as a timeless recluse in the mythical K'un-lun Mountains.

Chia Tao

185 *spirit through dreams:* It was thought that in dreams the spirit leaves the body and roams.

187 *Ch'i Li:* Ch'i Li-chi (3ʳᵈ–2ⁿᵈ c. B.C.E.) retired to the mountains and lived there as a recluse to protest the Ch'in Dynasty's tyranny.

188 *four patriarchs:* The first four Ch'an patriarchs.

Tu Mu

195 *Southern Dynasty:* A series of short-lived dynasties during the 5ᵗʰ and 6ᵗʰ centuries C.E., when northern China was controlled by "barbarians."

Mei Yao-ch'en

205 *8th Moon, 9th Sun:* See note to p. 152.

Crows . . . cry: The cry of crows was traditionally thought to be inauspicious.

207 *write out the year:* Mei would have written out the date, perhaps added a poem, and signed the inscription. In so doing, he would have both commemorated this illustrious visit and left behind a highly valued instance of his calligraphic art.

208 *garlic . . . dew:* There is an ancient burial song entitled *Dew on Garlic*, which was originally composed specifically for royalty.

209 *mirrors:* In ancient China, mirrors were made of polished bronze. They were typically round and so were, like roundcakes, appropriate for calling back the moon, which is itself often compared to a mirror.

Wang An-shih

219 *Dreams a ruins . . . :* Perhaps a reference to the fact that the dramatic social reforms that Wang An-shih had instituted as prime minister were largely dismantled by Wang's opponents after he retired.

220 *sweeping my gate-path:* A traditional gesture of welcome for anticipated visitors. See note to p. 9.

Su Tung-p'o

223 *Setting animals loose:* In their reverence for the sanctity of life, Buddhists would go to the markets, buy captured animals, and set them free.

225 *moonlight:* The pure clarity of moonlight is a common metaphor for the clarity of empty mind. Cf. p. 134.

226 *Yen Tzu-ling:* To avoid the necessity of serving in the government when his old friend became emperor in 25 C.E., Yen Tzu-ling disappeared into the mountains. He was found fishing at Seven-Mile Rapids, but refused the high offices that were offered him. Yen lived his life out as a recluse-farmer.

227 *Lady West:* Hsi Tzu or Hsi Shih, a great beauty from the 5th century B.C.E.

234 *Red Cliffs:* Site on the Yangtze where an epochal naval battle was fought in 208 C.E. In this battle, the crucial event in the collapse of the Han Dynasty, Lord Chou defeated the vastly superior fleet of the Han general Ts'ao Ts'ao by tangling it in a series of burning barges, thereby setting the Han fleet on fire. Twelve years later, the moribund Han fell, succeeded by the Three Kingdoms period (220–280).

236 This poem is said to record Su Tung-p'o's enlightenment, and has been an oft-cited part of the Ch'an literature ever since. The story is that Abbot Perpetua All-Gathering (Ch'ang-tsung) had given Su Tung-p'o a koan proposing that inanimate things continuously express Dharma. Su stayed up all night working on the koan, then at dawn wrote this poem as his answer. After reading it, the abbot acknowledged Su's awakening.

tongue . . . body: The Buddhist literature speaks of Buddha's "tongue broad and unending," Dharma's "body pure and clear," and the "eighty-four thousand" teachings of Buddha.

239 *Peach blossoms . . . Savage-Knoll: Peach blossoms drift streamwater away* refers to the Li Po poem on p. 80. The peach blossoms and Savage-Knoll (Wu-ling) refer to T'ao Ch'ien's famous "Peach-Blossom Spring" (see my translation, p. 70), which describes paradise as a secluded mountain village lost to the world and which is found by a fisherman at Savage-Knoll.

240 Written close to the end of Su Tung-p'o's life, on his journey back north after his exile on Hai-nan Island "beyond the sea."

Hui Neng's streamwater: Su Tung-p'o is at Hui Neng's monastery. See note to p. 121.

Lu Yu

245 *Little-Forest:* One of China's most famous monasteries, Little-Forest (Shao-lin) is said to be where Chinese martial arts originated and where Bodhidharma sat in meditation for nine years.

248 *palace lake:* K'un-ming Lake at the imperial palace in Ch'ang-an. Lu Yu lived during the Southern Sung, a period when northern China was controlled by "barbarians," and he never stopped lamenting the loss of northern China and Ch'ang-an, the traditional capital.

249 *Maker-of-Things:* See note to p. 152.

Yang Wan-li

264 *absolutely:* This is the same idea as in T'ao Ch'ien's famous "Drinking Wine #5," p. 13.

265 *Shu . . . Wu:* Ancient names for western and southeastern China.

Key Terms
An Outline of Wilderness Thought in Ancient China

Tao: 道 Way

Tao originally meant "way," as in "pathway" or "roadway," a meaning it has kept. But Lao Tzu and Chuang Tzu redefined it as a spiritual concept by using it to describe the generative ontological process (hence, a "Way") through which all things arise and pass away. As such, Tao can be divided into two aspects: being *(yu)*, the ten thousand living and nonliving things of the empirical world, and nonbeing *(wu)*, the generative source of being and its transformations. The Taoist way is to dwell as a part of this natural process. In that dwelling, self is but a fleeting form taken on by earth's process of change, or perhaps all and none of earth's fleeting forms simultaneously. But more absolutely, it is the emptiness of nonbeing, that source which endures through all change. See also: Introduction, p. xiv, and my translation of *Tao Te Ching,* pp. x and xvi ff.

> Ref: 34.14, 46.16, 48.7, 94.3, 129.1, 130.1, 137.1, 139.2, 172.5.

Tzu-jan: 自然 Occurrence appearing of itself

The literal meaning of *tzu-jan* is "self-ablaze." From this comes "self-so" or "the of-itself," which as a philosophical concept becomes "being such of itself," hence "spontaneous" or "natural." But a more revealing translation of *tzu-jan* might be "occurrence appearing of itself," for it is meant to describe the ten thousand things burgeoning forth spontaneously from the generative source, each according to its own nature, independent and self-sufficient, each dying and returning to the process of change, only to reappear in another self-generating form. Hence, *tzu-jan* might be described as the mechanism or process of Tao in the empirical world. See also: Introduction, p. xiv ff., and my translation of *Tao Te Ching,* pp. xx ff. and 95.

> Ref: 9.20, 25.7.

Wu-wei: 無為 Nothing's own doing, etc.

Impossible to translate the same way in every instance, *wu-wei* means acting as a spontaneous part of *tzu-jan* rather than with the self-conscious intention that seems to separate us from *tzu-jan*'s selfless process. Different contexts emphasize different aspects of this rich philosophical concept as writers exploit the term's grammat-ical ambiguity. Literally meaning "not/nothing *(wu)* doing *(wei)*," *wu-wei*'s most straightforward translation is simply "doing nothing" in the sense of not interfering with the flawless and self-sufficient unfolding of *tzu-jan*. But this must always be conceived together with its mirror translation: "nothing doing" or "nothing's own doing," in the sense of being no one separate from *tzu-jan* when acting. As *wu-wei* is the movement of *tzu-jan*, when we act according to *wu-*

wei we act as the generative source. This opens to the deepest level of this philosophical complex, for *wu-wei* can also be read quite literally as "nonbeing *(wu)* doing." Here, *wu-wei* action is action directly from, or indeed *as* the ontological source: nonbeing burgeoning forth into being. This in turn invests the more straightforward translation ("doing nothing") with its fullest dimensions, for "doing nothing" always carries the sense of "enacting nothing/nonbeing."

Although this central term does not itself occur in the poems of this anthology (but see the quote from *Chuang Tʒu* in note to p. 135), it is a constant presence as a spiritual posture that these poets aspired to and most enacted in their poetry, each in their own unique way.

Hsüan: 玄 Dark-enigma

Dark-Enigma came to have a particular philosophic resonance, for it became the name of a neo-Taoist school of philosophy in the 3ʳᵈ and 4ᵗʰ centuries C.E.: Dark-Enigma Learning, a school that gave Chinese thought a decidedly ontological turn and became central to the synthesis of Taoism and Buddhism into Ch'an Buddhism. Like Lao Tzu, the thinkers of the Dark-Enigma Learning school equated dark-enigma with nonbeing, the generative ontological tissue from which the ten thousand things spring. Or more properly, it is Way before it is named, before nonbeing and being give birth to one another—that region where consciousness and ontology share their source.

Ref: 46.14, 49.7, 155.4, 158.2, 171.10.

Li: 理 Inner pattern

The philosophical meaning of *li*, which originally referred to the veins and markings in a precious piece of jade, is something akin to what we call natural law. It is the system of principles that governs the unfolding of *tʒu-jan*. *Li* therefore weaves nonbeing and being into a single boundless tissue. But concepts at these ontological depths blur, especially in the intermingling of Taoist and Buddhist thought, and in the hands of various writers *li* appears virtually synonymous with a host of other key concepts: even Tao or *tʒu-jan*, and Buddha or *prājña* (the Buddhist term for enlightenment in which emptiness is understood to be the true nature of all things). This concept is especially important to the work of Hsieh Ling-yün and Su Tung-p'o, for which see the respective Introductions (pp. 20 and 221).

Ref: 18.10, 25.2, 34.13, 49.7, 73.7.

T'ien: 天 Heaven

From its primitive meaning of "sky," *heaven* became a kind of all-controlling deity in early Chinese culture. Although it always retains connotations of "sky," the early Taoist masters adapted this concept to mean "natural process," the constant unfolding of things in the process of *tzu-jan*, thereby giving it a sacred dimension. See also my translation of *Tao Te Ching*, pp. xiv, xix–xx, and 96.

Ref: passim.

Hsin: 心 Mind

In ancient China, there was no fundamental distinction between heart and mind: The term *hsin* connotes all that we think of in the two concepts together. This range of meaning often blends into the technical use of *hsin* in Taoism and Ch'an Buddhism, where it means consciousness emptied of all content, or perhaps consciousness as empty awareness. The recurring terms "empty mind" and "no-mind" emphasize this meaning. And at this fundamental level, mind is nothing other than nonbeing, the pregnant void from which all things are engendered.

Ref: passim.

K'ung: 空 Emptiness

This concept resonates in a number of Taoist and Buddhist ways. In general it is vaguely synonymous with nonbeing, that pregnant emptiness that underlies the ever-changing manifestations of being. As such it is often used in describing mind. When used in reference to the empirical world, it suggests that the ten thousand things are most fundamentally nonbeing, and so "empty." From this follows the ecological principle that all things arise in their particular forms from the web of being (infused as it is with nonbeing), then dissolve back into it as the material that will reappear in future forms. Hence, there is no permanent selfhood.

Ref: passim.

Hsien: 閒 Idleness

Etymologically, the character for idleness that T'ao Ch'ien used *(hsien)* connotes "profound serenity and quietness," its pictographic elements rendering moonlight (empty mind: cf. note to p. 225) shining through open gates (awareness: cf. note to p. 9). Later, another character was also used: *lan*. The pictographic elements of this character are equally revealing: It is made up of the character for "trust" beside the character for "heart-mind." Hence, the heart-mind of trust, the heart-mind of trust in the world. But this is trust of truly profound dimensions, for "idleness" is essentially a lazybones word for the spiritual posture known as *wu-wei*. Hence, idleness is a kind of meditative reveling in *tzu-jan*, a state in which daily life becomes the essence of spiritual practice.

Ref: passim.

Finding List

Page	1. *Meng Hao-jan Chi*	2. *Meng Hao-jan Shih Chi Chien Chu*
42	1.12a	329
43	3.6b	152
44		419
45	1.7a	246
46	1.1b	11
47	1.10a	6
48	3.8b	140
49	3.5a	375
50	1.2b	52
51	2.1a	86
52	3.3a	32
53	4.11b	338
54	3.5a	87
55	4.7a	66
56	1.12a	75

Wang Wei

1. *Wang Yu-ch'eng Chi Chu*. Chao Tien-ch'eng, ed. 1736. SPPY (*chüan* and page number).

2. *Wang Yu-ch'eng Chi Chien Chu*. Chao Tien-ch'eng, ed. 1961 (page number).

Page	1. *Wang Yu-ch'eng Chi Chu*	2. *Wang Yu-ch'eng Chi Chien Chu*
58	13.12a	256
59	13.1a	239
60	13.2b	241
67	13.1a	239
68	7.3b	118
69	14.7a	266
70	13.1b	240
71	9.1a	153
72	7.6b	123
73	7.4b	120

Li Po

1. *Li T'ai-po Shih Chi*. Wang Chi, ed. 1759. SPPY (*chüan* and page number).

2. *Li Po Chi Chiao Chu*. Ch'ü Shui-yüan, ed. 1980 (page number).

Page	1. *Li T'ai-po Shih Chi*	2. *Li Po Chi Chiao Chu*
75	20.9a	1170
76	21.11a	1238

78	15.15b	935
79	22.14b	1299
80	19.2b	1095
81	23.2b	1331
82	21.5a	1222
83	24.21a	1422
84	23.8a	1349
85	23.10a	1354
86	23.10a	1354
87	8.1a	533
88	24.19b	1416
89	20.22b	1207
90	22.21a	1316
91	30.11a	1715
92	8.16b	579
93	23.9a	1350
94	6.9b	443

TU FU

1. *Chiu Chia Chi Chu Tu Shih*. Kuo Chih-ta, ed. 1183. In William Hung's *A Concordance to the Poetry of Tu Fu*. 1940 (*chüan* and poem number).

2. *Tu Shih Ching Ch'uan*. Yang Lun, ed. 1791 (*chüan* and page number).

Page	1. *Chih Chia Chi Chu Tu Shih*	2. *Tu Shih Ching Ch'uan*
97	1/5	1.1a
98	17/14	1.2a
99	20/11	6.11a
100	21/25	7.29b
101	31/44	12.25b
102	29/14	13.13b
103	30/32	13.22b
104	31/34	15.10a
105	32/25	15.24a
106	31/35	17.11b
107	30/6	14.4b
108	30/29	17.15b
109	32/29	17.16a
110	32/3	17.18a
111	30/34	17.1a
112	32/28	17.33b
113	32/12	17.34a
115	34/6	19.4b

WEI YING-WU

1. *Wei Su-chou Chi*. SPPY (*chüan* and page number).
2. *Wei Ying-wu Chi Chia Chu*. T'ao Min and Wang Yu-sheng, eds. 1998 (page number).

Page	1. *Wei Su-chou Chi*	2. *Wei Ying-wu Chi Chia Chu*
117	7.4b	427
118	8.11b	533
119	3.10b	194
120	7.7a	442
121	7.12b	474
122	8.11a	530
123	7.5b	433
124	3.8a	173
125	7.11b	468
126	7.12b	473
127	7.12a	470

COLD MOUNTAIN (HAN SHAN)

Poem numbers follow numbering in *Han Shan Tzu Shih Chi* and *Ch'üan T'ang Shih*. Depending on the edition of *Ch'üan T'ang Shih* consulted, the Cold Mountain collection is found either in *chüan* 860 or *han* 12, *ts'e* 1, *chüan* 1.

MENG CHIAO

1. *Meng Tung-yeh Shih Chi*. Hua Ch'en-chih, ed. 1959 (page number).
2. *Meng Tung-yeh Chi*. SPPY (*chüan* and page number).
3. *Meng Tung-yeh Shih Chu*. Ch'en Yen-chieh, ed. 1939 (*chüan* and page number).

Page	1. *Meng Tung-yeh Shih Chi*	2. *Meng Tung-yeh Chi*	3. *Meng Tung-yeh Shih Chu*
143	185	10.4b	10.6a
147	58	4.1a	4.1a

LIU TSUNG-YÜAN

1. *Liu Ho-tung Chi*. 1961 (page number).
2. *Liu Ho-tung Ch'üan Chi*. SPPY (*chüan* and page number).

Page	1. *Liu Ho-tung Chi*	2. *Liu Ho-tung Ch'üan Chi*
151	724	43.13a
152	470	29.2b
154	725	43.14a
155	672	42.17b

156	707	42.27a
157	740	43.25b
158	703	42.24b
159	692	42.17a

Po Chü-i

1. *Po Chü-i Chi Chien Chiao.* Chu Chin-ch'eng, ed. 1988 (page number).
2. *Po Chü-i Chi.* Ku Hsüeh-chieh, ed. 1979 (page number).
3. *Po Hsiang-shan Shih Chi.* Wang Li-ming, ed. SPPY. 1703 (*chüan* and page number).

Page	1. *Po Chü-i Chi Chien Chiao*	2. *Po Chü-i Chi*	3. *Po Hsiang-shan Shih Chi*
161	498	179	9.7b
162	725	251	13.5a
163	302	103	5.7b
164	857	290	14.11a
165	355	126	6.11a
166	384	137	7.6a
168	1028	342	16.11b
169	1031	343	16.12b
170	624	225	11.10b
171	448	161	21.5a
172	1904	620	31.1b
173	1954	637	30.6b
174	2062	678	24.3b
175	2169	715	32.13a
176	2485	822	24.15b
178	2487	823	24.16a

Chia Tao

1. *Ch'ang Chiang Chi.* SPPY (*chüan* and page number).
2. *Chia Tao Shih Chu.* Ch'en Yen-chieh, ed. 1937 (page number).

Page	1. *Ch'ang Chiang Chi*	2. *Chia Tao Shih Chu*
180	3.2b	29
181		
182	6.6a	76
183	6.3b	72
184	10.5a	124
185	3.3b	32
186	10.1a	115
187	6.3b	71
188	9.3b	110

TU MU

1. *Fan-ch'uan Shih Chi Chu.* SPPY (*chüan* and page number; w indicates the *wai-pien* section).

Page	1. *Fan-ch'uan Shih Chi Chu*
190	3.26a
191	4.10b
192	4.7b
193	w.8b
194	4.31b
195	3.7b
196	4.17b
197	4.31a
198	2.16a
199	3.14a

MEI YAO-CH'EN

1. *Wan-ling Chi.* SPPY (*chüan* and page number).

Page	1. *Wan-ling Chi*
204	43.7a
205	36.4b
206	7.6a
208	7.3a
209	19.1a

WANG AN-SHIH

1. *Lin-chuan Chi.* SPPY (*chüan* and page number).
2. *Chien Chu Wang Ching-kung Shih (Wang Ching-kung Shih Chu).* Li Pi, ed. 1214 (page number and *chüan*).

Page	1. *Lin-chuan Chi*	2. *Chien Chu Wang Ching-kung Shih*
211	30.10a	1155 (47)
212	28.8b	1028 (42)
213	30.8b	1087 (44)
214	27.6a	992 (41)
215	29.5a	1043 (43)
216	30.5a	1070 (44)
217	31.7b	1106 (45)
218	14.7a	564 (22)
219	30.5b	1074 (44)
220	27.6a	992 (41)

SU TUNG-P'O

1. *Su Shih Shih Chi*. Feng Ying-liu and Wang Wen-kao, eds. 1982 (page number and *chüan*).
2. *Tung-p'o Ch'i Chi*. Ch'eng Tsung, ed. SPPY (collection, *chüan*, and page number; *Chi* = *Tung-p'o Chi* and *Hsü* = *Tung-p'o Hsü Chi*).
3. *Ch'üan Sung Tz'u*. T'ang Kuei-chang, ed. 1940 (page number).
4. *Su Tung-p'o Tz'u*. Ts'ao Shu-ming, ed. 1968 (poem number).

Page	1. *Su Shih Shih Chi*	2. *Tung-p'o Ch'i Chi*	3. *Ch'üan Sung Tz'u*	4. *Su Tung-p'o Tz'u*
222	183 (4)	*Chi* 2.4a		
223	339 (7)	*Chi* 3.6b		
225	380 (8)	*Chi* 4.1a		
226			303	3
227	430 (9)	*Chi* 4.7a		
228	547 (11)	*Chi* 6.3a		
229	580 (12)	*Chi* 6.5b		
230	584 (12)	*Chi* 6.6a		
231	872 (17)	*Chi* 10.1b		
232	951 (18)	*Chi* 11.5a		
233	985 (19)	*Chi* 6.3a		
234			282	130
235			288	150
236	1218 (23)	*Chi* 13.10b		
237	1219 (23)	*Chi* 13.10b		
238	1607 (30)	*Chi* 17.9b		
240	2426 (45)	*Hsü* 2.12b		

LU YU

1. *Lu Fang-weng Ch'üan Chi*. SPPY (*chüan* and page number).

Page	1. *Lu Fang-weng Ch'üan Chi*
242	63.1a
243	63.1b
244	63.1b
245	63.1b
246	63.2a
247	63.2a
248	63.2a
249	63.2a

FAN CH'ENG-TA

1. *Fan Shih-hu Chi.* Chou Ju-ch'ang, ed. 1974 (page number and *chüan*).

Page	1. *Fan Shih-hu Chi*
251	274 (19)
252	372 (27)

YANG WAN-LI

1. *Ch'eng-chai Shih Chi.* SPPY (*chüan* and page number).

Page	1. *Ch'eng-chai Shih Chi*
258	2.6a
259	12.3a
260	12.7a
261	14.4a
262	16.4b
263	20.6b
264	28.12b
266	31.8a
267	34.5a
268	8.2b
269	35.11b

Selected Reading

For poets I have translated, I list only my books because they are the next place to go after the selections in this volume. For readers wanting to investigate the poets in more depth, those books contain extensive bibliographies.

GENERAL

Chün Shih. *Chung-Kuo Shan-Shui T'ien-Yüan Shih Tzu Hsüan*. 1965.

Nienhauser, William. *The Indiana Companion to Traditional Chinese Literature.* Bloomington: Indiana University Press, 1986.

Owen, Stephen. *Traditional Chinese Poetry and Poetics.* Madison: University of Wisconsin Press, 1985.

Strassberg, Richard. *Inscribed Landscapes: Travel Writing from Imperial China.* Berkeley: University of California Press, 1994.

Yüan Hsing-pei and Chang Hsiang-ju. *Chung-Kuo Shan-Shui Shih Hsüan.* 1983.

INTRODUCTION

Cheng, François. *Chinese Poetic Writing: With an Anthology of T'ang Poetry.* Donald Riggs and J. P. Seaton, trans. Bloomington: Indiana University Press, 1982.

Chuang Tzu. *Chuang Tzu: The Inner Chapters.* David Hinton, trans. Washington, D.C.: Counterpoint Press, 1997.

Frodsham, J. D. "The Origins of Chinese Nature Poetry," *Asia Major,* 8.1 (1960), 68–104.

Lao Tzu. *Tao Te Ching.* David Hinton, trans. Washington, D.C.: Counterpoint Press, 2000.

T'AO CH'IEN

T'ao Ch'ien. *The Selected Poems of T'ao Ch'ien.* David Hinton, trans. Port Townsend, Wash.: Copper Canyon Press, 1993.

HSIEH LING-YÜN

Hsieh Ling-yün. *The Mountain Poems of Hsieh Ling-yün.* David Hinton, trans. New York: New Directions, 2001.

T'ANG DYNASTY

Owen, Stephen. *The Great Age of Chinese Poetry: The High T'ang.* New Haven: Yale University Press, 1981.

MENG HAO-JAN

Meng Hao-jan. *The Mountain Poems of Meng Hao-jan.* David Hinton, trans. New York: Archipelago Books, 2004.

Wang Wei

Wagner, Marsha. *Wang Wei*. Boston: Twyane Publishers, 1982.

Wang Wei. *Hiding the Universe: Poems by Wang Wei*. Wai-lim Yip, trans. New York: Grossman, 1972.

_____. *Laughing Lost in the Mountains: Poems of Wang Wei*. Tony Barnstone, Willis Barnstone, Xu Haixin, trans. Hanover: University Press of New England, 1991.

Yu, Pauline. *The Poetry of Wang Wei: New Translations and Commentary*. Bloomington: Indiana University Press, 1980.

Li Po

Li Po. *The Selected Poems of Li Po*. David Hinton, trans. New York: New Directions, 1996.

Tu Fu

Tu Fu. *The Selected Poems of Tu Fu*. David Hinton, trans. New York: New Directions, 1989.

Cold Mountain (Han Shan)

Cold Mountain. *Cold Mountain: 100 Poems by the T'ang Poet Han-shan*. Burton Watson, trans. New York: Grove Press, 1962. Reprint New York: Columbia University Press, 1970.

_____. *The Collected Songs of Cold Mountain*. Red Pine, trans. Port Townsend, Wash.: Copper Canyon Press, 1983. Revised edition, 2000.

_____. *The Poetry of Han-Shan: A Complete, Annotated Translation of Cold Mountain*. Robert Henricks, trans. Albany: State University of New York Press, 1990.

Snyder, Gary. *Riprap and Cold Mountain Poems*. San Francisco: Four Seasons Foundation, 1969. Reprint Berkeley: North Point Press, 1990.

Waley, Arthur. *Chinese Poems*. London: George Allen & Unwin, 1946.

Meng Chiao

Meng Chiao. *The Late Poems of Meng Chiao*. David Hinton, trans. Princeton: Princeton University Press, 1996.

Liu Tsung-yüan

Nienhauser, William, et al. *Liu Tsung-yüan*. New York: Twayne Publishers, 1973.

Strassberg, Richard. *Inscribed Landscapes*.

Po Chü-i

Po Chü-i. *The Selected Poems of Po Chü-i*. David Hinton, trans. New York: New Directions, 1999.

_____. *Selected Poems*. Burton Watson, trans. New York: Columbia University Press, 2000.

CHIA TAO

Chia Tao. *When I Find You Again It Will Be in Mountains.* Mike O'Connor, trans. Somerville, Mass.: Wisdom Publications, 2000.

SUNG DYNASTY

Yoshikawa, Kojiro. *An Introduction to Sung Poetry.* Cambridge: Harvard University Press, 1967.

MEI YAO-CH'EN

Chaves, Jonathan. *Mei Yao-ch'en and the Development of Early Sung Poetry.* New York: Columbia University Press, 1976.

SU TUNG-P'O

Egan, Ronald. *Word, Image, and Deed in the Life of Su Shi.* Cambridge: Harvard University Press, 1994.

Fuller, Michael. *The Road to East Slope: The Development of Su Shi's Poetic Voice.* Stanford: Stanford University Press, 1990.

Grant, Beata. *Mount Lu Revisited: Buddhism in the Life and Writings of Su Shih.* Honolulu: University of Hawaii Press, 1994.

Lin, Yutang. *The Gay Genius: The Life and Times of Su Tungpo.* New York: John Day, 1947.

Strassberg, Richard. *Inscribed Landscapes.*

Su Tung-p'o. *Selected Poems of Su Tung-p'o.* Burton Watson, trans. Port Townsend, Wash.: Copper Canyon Press, 1994.

LU YU

Duke, Michael. *Lu You.* Boston: Twayne Publishers, 1977.

Lu Yu. *The Old Man Who Does as He Pleases.* Burton Watson, trans. New York: Columbia University Press, 1973.

FAN CH'ENG-TA

Hargett, James. "Boulder Lake Poems: Fan Chengda's (1126–1193) Rural Year in Suzhou Revisited," *Chinese Literature: Essays, Articles, Reviews,* 10.1–2 (1988), 109–131.

Schmidt, J. D. *Stone Lake: The Poetry of Fan Chengda, 1126–1193.* Cambridge: Cambridge University Press, 1992.

YANG WAN-LI

Schmidt, J. D. *Yang Wan-li.* New York: Twayne Publishers, 1976.

Yang Wan-li. *Heaven My Blanket, Earth My Pillow.* Jonathan Chaves, trans. New York: Weatherhill, 1975.

Acknowledgments

Grateful acknowledgment is made for permission to reprint from my previous books the selections representing the following poets:

T'ao Ch'ien: Copper Canyon Press (The Selected Poems of T'ao Ch'ien)

Hsieh Ling-yün: New Directions Publishing (The Mountain Poems of Hsieh Ling-yün)

Li Po: New Directions Publishing (The Selected Poems of Li Po)

Tu Fu: New Directions Publishing (The Selected Poems of Tu Fu)

Meng Chiao: Princeton University Press (The Late Poems of Meng Chiao)

Po Chü-i: New Directions Publishing (The Selected Poems of Po Chü-i)

New Directions Paperbooks—A Partial Listing

For a complete listing request free catalog from New Directions, 80 Eighth Avenue,
New York 10011; or visit our website, www.ndpublishing.com

†Bilingual

For a complete listing request free catalog from New Directions, 80 Eighth Avenue
New York 10011; or go visit our website, www.ndpublishing.com

†Bilingual